# Invisible Capital

Few tricks of the unsophisticated intellect are more curious than the naive psychology of the business man, who ascribes his achievements to his own unaided efforts, in bland unconsciousness of a social order without whose continuous support and vigilant protection he would be as a lamb bleating in the desert.

R.H. Tawney, *Religion and the Rise of Capitalism*
(1922)

# Invisible Capital

## How Unseen Forces Shape
## Entrepreneurial Opportunity

**CHRIS RABB**

Berrett–Koehler Publishers, Inc.
San Francisco
*a BK Currents book*

Berrett-Koehler Publishers, Inc.
235 Montgomery Street, Suite 650
San Francisco, CA 94104-2916
Tel: (415) 288-0260    Fax: (415) 362-2512
www.bkconnection.com

Ordering Information
**Quantity sales.** Special discounts are available on quantity purchases by corporations, associa-
tions, and others. For details, contact the "Special Sales Department" at the Berrett-Koehler
address above.
**Individual sales.** Berrett-Koehler publications are available through most bookstores. They can
also be ordered directly from Berrett-Koehler: Tel: (800) 929-2929; Fax: (802) 864-7626;
www.bkconnection.com.
**Orders for college textbook/course adoption use.** Please contact Berrett-Koehler:
Tel: (800) 929-2929; Fax: (802) 864-7626.
**Orders by U.S. trade bookstores and wholesalers.** Please contact Ingram Publisher Services:
Tel: (800) 509-4887; Fax: (800) 838-1149; E-mail: customer.service@ingrampublisherservices.
com; or visit www.ingrampublisherservices.com/Ordering for details about electronic ordering.

Berrett-Koehler and the BK logo are registered trademarks of Berrett-Koehler Publishers, Inc.

Printed in the United States of America

Berrett-Koehler books are printed on long-lasting acid-free paper. When it is available, we
choose paper that has been manufactured by environmentally responsible processes. These
may include using trees grown in sustainable forests, incorporating recycled paper, minimizing
chlorine in bleaching, or recycling the energy produced at the paper mill.

**Library of Congress Cataloging-in-Publication Data**
Rabb, Chris.
Invisible capital : how unseen forces shape entrepreneurial opportunity / Chris Rabb. -- 1st ed.
    p. cm.
"Published in association with Demos."
Includes index.
ISBN 978-1-60509-307-9 (paperback : alk. paper)
1. Entrepreneurship. 2. Success in business. 3. Opportunity. I. Title.
HB615.R25 2010
338'.04--dc22
            2010034780

First Edition
14  13  12  11  10          10 9 8 7 6 5 4 3 2 1

Project management, design, and composition by Steven Hiatt / Hiatt & Dragon,
San Francisco    Copyediting: Mark Rhynsburger    Proofreading: Tom Hassett
Illustrations: Erin Shigaki    Cover design: Ian Shimkoviak / The Book Designers

# Contents

To the burgeoning enterprises dearest to me,
the precious lives of my sons, Freeman Diallo and Issa.
There is no greater wealth than the joy and pride
of being your daddy.

# Preface

There are any number of "How to succeed in business" books. Even more books tell you *how* various people have already succeeded in business. But very few books honestly address *why* some entrepreneurs succeed—and others don't. Still fewer even challenge the notion of success itself in this context.

Take Donald Trump, perhaps one of the best-known businessmen in modern times. In *Trump 101*,[1] "The Donald," as he is popularly known, tells readers they can succeed if they "tough it out," "listen to your gut," and "take chances." What he doesn't tell them is that they will have a better chance to succeed in the real estate business if real estate *is* the family business, if they work in the family business before venturing out on their own, if they have access to the right connections in that world, and if they know how to look, talk, and act once they start operating in that world.

Success comes easier if you start with capital—not just cold, hard cash, but a kind of hidden capital most people don't even know they have. Donald Trump spent his first five years in business working with his father, Fred Trump. He learned the art of the deal from his dad. He learned from his father the elements of success that few books can teach you—from what jokes to tell to where he would have the most success with different types of people (in the office, at a restaurant, or on the golf course). The young Donald could get his calls answered just by saying he was Fred Trump's son. That's invisible capital.

You and I have invisible capital of all kinds. Our cultural background, occupation, age, gender, educational training, and sexuality give us entree to some social groups—and may make it more difficult for us to enter others. Where you went to school, whether your parents were in business, what neighborhood you lived in as a child—all these factors can either propel you further or hold you back.

I saw the workings of invisible capital when I served as a legislative aide in the U.S. Senate. Each summer, interns would flood our offices, most of them recent college graduates. Among those interns were Congressional fellows who had received stipends to allow them to live and work on Capitol Hill for the summer. These prized fellowship opportunities were few and far between—and the process was therefore highly selective. As a result, they often went to talented college students whose parents or other adults in their lives had strong ties to one or more members of Congress or their senior staffers. These relationships exemplified the mantra of one of my earliest professional mentors, who would often say, "Network or not work!"—and who also, and not so coincidentally, was the benefactor of my very first corporate internship as a college freshman.

These young collegians all had enough invisible capital to secure fellowships to work on the Hill. But when autumn arrived and their stipends ended, they virtually all disappeared when no entry-level jobs in members' offices were available. Most of them could not find work elsewhere in Washington and were forced to go back where they came from despite their newfound connections, skills, and work experience.

One summer, however, I noticed that an intern who was not affiliated with that fellowship program continued working in our office even though there were no new job openings that fall. I learned later that she came from an upper-middle-class family that was both able and willing to support her while she sought employment on the Hill. In the interim, she continued working diligently as an unpaid intern in our office, building up her skills and connections within and beyond our office—just as the fellows had done, but over a longer period of time. When a job finally became available in our office, she was hired on the spot, even though at that time (during a recession) she was competing with job applicants who had more work experience and formal education than she had.

That is the essence of invisible capital. This young woman had been able to leverage invisible assets. One of those assets was the wealth of her family. But the story goes deeper. Her parents had made the strategic decision to bankroll her through the fall because they knew how the system worked, having gotten the scoop from several colleagues and relatives over the years. Most of the fellows came from high-income households with professional, college-educated parents. But they did not all share the same social networks—networks that when tapped into afforded them specialized knowledge, insights, and opportunities that their parental peers did not benefit from. Both sets of parents had invisible capital, but of a different composition and value based on the needs of the situation at hand.

Clearly, the unpaid intern would not have succeeded if she hadn't worked hard or was unruly or incompetent. Working hard matters. But what made the difference for her in terms of upward mobility was the interplay of these unseen forces.

It is noteworthy to mention here, for a number of interrelated reasons, that the unpaid intern was White and that her paid summer counterparts were Black and the recipients of Congressional Black Caucus Foundation fellowships. While employment discrimination is still rampant in the labor market,[2] in this example based on a very real scenario, race was not a factor—not a direct one, anyway.

Invisible capital is not a euphemism for whiteness or, for that matter, any of the other dominant statuses in society such as maleness, a high income, advanced education, occupational prestige, place of birth, or heterosexuality. However, there is a direct link from invisible capital to the opportunities and advantages that all these factors so often confer.[3]

The intern in my office did not get the job because she was White, nor because she was necessarily a harder worker or more intelligent than her counterparts in the fellowship program. She got the job because of the kind of invisible capital she acquired through her family. The summer interns did not lack invisible capital. It was not a matter of rich versus poor, or educated versus uneducated. In this situation, the networks that were strong enough to secure these fellows the opportunity to work as interns in Congress were still not enough to compensate for the specialized knowledge of the Capitol Hill job market that so greatly advantaged the unpaid intern. That knowledge was a direct benefit of the networks to which her parents had access, networks that were born of opportunities in environments that until the late 1960s were virtually inaccessible to communities of color and to women.

Nevertheless, the fellowship program is a modestly successful initiative despite its nontrivial structural flaw. It provides consistent summer employment opportunities for African Americans who are still woefully underrepresented at virtually every level of participation on Capitol Hill. However, it is that fundamental design flaw that allows one form of invisible capital to trump the kind that successful fellowship applicants have leveraged to make it to Washington, D.C., though they rarely stay when the summer internship comes to an end.[4]

The lesson here is that "no good deed goes unpunished"—if it fails to adequately challenge the assumptions inspired by prevailing myths around how to succeed in society. If intelligent, well-intentioned nonprofit managers can fall for this mythology, so can you, as you try to assess what it takes to excel in business. Too many people read "how-to-succeed" books and try to start a business without understanding what they really will need to survive and thrive. Like many newly minted (also referred to as "nascent") entrepreneurs, the young summer interns were quite successful in starting their journey on Capitol Hill, but when it came to expanding their opportunities after the fellowship, they came up short.

If you haven't surmised it by now, this book is not going to give you a simple recipe for success, nor will it show you how to make a million dollars in thirty days or while working in your pajamas. But if you've been paying attention so far, you've probably already gleaned some insight into how you must change the framework through which you process how we define, improve, and expand entrepreneurial opportunities for all.

And the "we" here is all of us who believe (or would like to think) that some more enlightened approach to expanding entrepreneurial opportunity will benefit not just ourselves or our loved ones, but entire communities.

This book is about invisible capital, and how invisible capital shapes the entrepreneurial gauntlet and influences the quality of entrepreneurship experienced by new and prospective practitioners who may have the necessary passion and perseverance, but lack the insight and perspective to adequately gauge the terrain they must navigate as entrepreneurs and business owners. *Invisible Capital* reveals the context in which businesses operate, grow or stagnate, flourish or falter. It shows what it will take to level a playing field that so privileges those with the most invisible capital.

One of the main messages of invisible capital is that entrepreneurs don't succeed on their own. So *Invisible Capital* is also for people who care about whether entrepreneurs succeed—and that's all of us, even those of us who do not consider ourselves entrepreneurial, business savvy, or particularly profit hungry.

What I learned from managing the entrepreneurial programs for a business assistance organization in an inner-city community was that the hardworking residents of these neighborhoods needed help operating on a playing field that does not tilt in their favor. It is a precarious plane not navigable by the faint of heart or those invested primarily in the "rags to riches" mythology. (I refer to the mythology that so many Americans, whether newly immigrated or descendants of multiple generations here, have so deeply internalized through what I describe later in this book as the Entrepreneurial-Industrial

Complex.) Our efforts to help poor and working-class people become entrepreneurs fail when we don't take into account the invisible, often society-wide barriers to success. To create a truly democratic marketplace, we need to understand what invisible capital these folks bring to the table—and what they lack. When we radically improve entrepreneurial literacy, we will be better able to design more comprehensive business assistance programs for the next generation of American entrepreneurs.

Entrepreneurship is about much more than money. Entrepreneurs bring innovation and opportunity to the table. Entrepreneurs build wealth, create jobs, and bring us new products, services, technologies, processes—even new ways of thinking. The businesses they create are not just financially profitable, but offer the possibility for our whole society to profit. When someone starts a hair salon in an inner-city neighborhood and employs local residents to cut hair, the entire neighborhood profits. When an entrepreneur devises a new seat for bicycles so that women can safely bike their children to day care, the whole community—and the environment—profits. Entrepreneurship done well can create profits with principles.

My passion for entrepreneurship is personal. I come from a family of entrepreneurs and have spent my professional life working to understand the impact of entrepreneurship on our economy and society at large. After working in the U.S. Senate, I went on to join the staff of the White House Conference on Small Business as writer, researcher, and trainer, and there I coordinated lively panels of entrepreneurial experts and business owners from all walks of life. The White House Conference was a nonpartisan federal commission tasked by the 103rd Congress to gauge the status and concerns of "Small Business America," having been inaugurated in 1980 by an act of Congress and resuscitated in 1986, and again, most recently, in 1994.[5]

For a brief time, I worked for a small, local chamber of commerce in Chicago, and years later ran a nationally acclaimed business incubator in Philadelphia. I also have real-life experience as an entrepreneur. I helped raise a quarter million dollars to fund a high-tech product design firm I founded with my older brother—an inventor, engineer, and gifted computer scientist.

When it comes to entrepreneurship, I've been involved in this ecosystem in a range of highly complementary roles that have given me practical, policy, and programmatic perspectives on this important subject. I've also advised entrepreneurs as a consultant and served on the board of directors of two family-owned businesses, including one that spans three centuries and five generations—a regional newspaper acquired by one of my great-great-grandfathers in the 1890s.

*Invisible Capital* reflects all of these experiences. I draw on the latest research on American entrepreneurship, including the Kauffman Firm Survey, the Panel on the Study of Entrepreneurial Development (PSED), and scholarship based on U.S. Census data to show how entrepreneurship really works in this country—who tries, who succeeds, and why broad-based success matters to our nation as a whole.

I offer up fictionalized examples of the real-life issues faced by many entrepreneurs. And I bring to the table my own experience as an entrepreneur and the years of hard work I put into my own business ventures, which give me a practical sense of which assumptions are well founded and which ones aren't.

The Introduction explains what invisible capital is and how it shapes entrepreneurial failure and success. You will learn why hard work and a great idea are important, but not sufficient, to achieve success, and what you can do about that. In chapter 1, I start with my own tragic assumptions about what I thought it took to start, fund, and grow a business, which leads into a broader description of the challenges that await most prospective business owners. It is essentially an exposition of the difference between the ease of starting a business and the radically harder endeavor of keeping one afloat.

Chapter 2 explores the landscape of modern American enterprise. This chapter will give you a brief overview of the composition and performance of U.S. businesses. What does it take to be an entrepreneur? In chapter 3, I explain how invisible capital operates, using composite cases and other illustrative examples to make these theoretical ideas real. It's the best chapter to read to truly understand how to assess your own invisible capital: to inventory what you already have, and to learn what you need—or, for that matter, learn what your colleagues, clients, peers, or loved ones need.

Why don't we know more about invisible capital? In chapter 4, I examine all the different things that explain how and why we seem to know so little about something Americans seem to value so much: striking out on our own in search of greater independence and good fortune. Drawing on numerous scholarly studies, I argue that the very governmental and other programs designed to help entrepreneurs don't seem to know where to start to level the playing field; as a result they so often come up short by overlooking the unique value of thoughtfully merging democratic opportunity with entrepreneurial advancement.

In chapter 5, I offer solutions. Here are practical steps and measures we can take to systematically enable entrepreneurs to achieve success—starting with reshaping how we define entrepreneurial success, both for ourselves as entrepreneurs and as members of communities in which we are deeply invested.

Chapter 6 shows what those of us who do not self-identify as entrepreneurs can do to support and promote the growth of what I call "commonwealth enterprises" and the new, amazing breed of enlightened entrepreneurs who will be at their helm. I sum up what we must keep in mind as we expose the role of invisible capital and advance the kind of entrepreneurship we so desperately need more of. And though "doing good while doing well" is great, I believe doing good *for, with,* and *in* our communities might just help us do well! Quite well, and in ways that matter most to us as interconnected people—not just as individual consumers.

We face a crisis of entrepreneurial illiteracy in our country—not just among the ordinary people who want to become entrepreneurs, but even among the politicians and leaders who promote entrepreneurship. Too many think tanks and business books act as if all it takes to achieve entrepreneurial success is to follow the Yellow Brick

Road of hard work. Make it to Oz and, like Dorothy, you will get what you want. That story of entrepreneurship would be great if it were true. But it's not. It's time to pull the curtain aside and see how invisible capital really works. Entrepreneurs need this knowledge to build their own success. Moreover, our communities need this knowledge to understand how our fragile economy actually works—and what can help where we need help the most.

Invisibility always protects someone. We also need to draw the curtain aside to make sure that a small group of people do not benefit unfairly by claiming their success came from hard work when it was actually a combination of work and the gift of privilege, be it inborn or acquired. Just by revealing the workings of invisible capital, we make democratizing entrepreneurial opportunity that much more possible and level a playing field that too few of us even realize is not flat. The better we understand the workings of invisible capital, the better we will be able to address equalizing its effects. We have the power to better align our individual and collective goals by promoting community-centered enterprises that draw from and contribute to local economies rather than continuing to reflexively validate a "growth for growth's sake," consumption-stunted mind-set.

*Chris Rabb*
*Philadelphia*
*August 2010*

# Introduction

We Americans today dream a very powerful and exciting dream. In this dream, a young man with a good attitude, a great idea, and a willingness to work hard starts a little business. That business grows and grows until the still-young founder is able to leave the day-to-day operations to his paid staff while he enjoys the good life: big mansions, Caribbean beachside villas, luxury cars, and beautiful companions. We call this story a "dream" because we know in our guts that it's not real. Very few entrepreneurs will create businesses that are profitable, let alone businesses that will be able to hire employees. Most businesses have no employees, and most of them will never have employees. Many businesses are "side hustles," glorified hobbies that will never grow. Just over one in four businesses actually brings in enough revenue to hire paid staff,[1] which explains why the average number of employees per U.S. firm—with or without a payroll—is just four![2] Just 2 percent of all businesses have employees, with large corporations being overrepresented as private employers of our nation's massive workforce.

Even among those businesses that do hire employees, only about one in ten hire twenty or more workers. And the average employee count per "employer-firm"? Around twenty.

Depending on what survey you read, at least half of all businesses are home based, and over 70 percent are sole proprietorships. Most of these business owners are working hard every day, often seven days a week. They *are* their business. Or, to put it another way, they are not out driving around in their Ferraris, as the late-night infomercials would have us believe.

## We Don't Need More Entrepreneurs, We Need Better Entrepreneurs

Too often our media and politicians divide our economic world into "big business" and "small business." In our culture, we tend to think that the dividing line is drawn between massive businesses like Citicorp or General Motors and little "mom and pop" businesses. The Small Business Administration (SBA), however, generally defines small businesses as any U.S. "nonfarm, for-profit" firm with fewer than 500 employees.[3] That means that TiVo, until recently, was a small business, since it fell below this arbitrary employee threshold.

When you close your eyes and think of a small business, does TiVo come to mind? Not likely, yet the company whose name has become an indispensable verb in millions of homes across the country was until recently a "small business" when applying the most generic SBA standard of proof. In fact, by this definition, 99 percent of all businesses in America are technically small businesses. The definition is so large as to be pointless. The real line of demarcation shouldn't distinguish between big and small, but between those that are sustainable and produce a broad net impact on our society and those that do not. After all, we may operate in an economy composed of markets, but we live in a society made up of communities.

This book is about building those real businesses, businesses that will grow to hire employees but may never have more than twenty paid staff. What matters about these businesses is that they become sustainable and bolster local economies and the communities they operate in.

When pundits say that we need new businesses to create jobs, they are rarely telling the whole story. Creating new businesses is a good idea, but the jobs they create have been historically fleeting

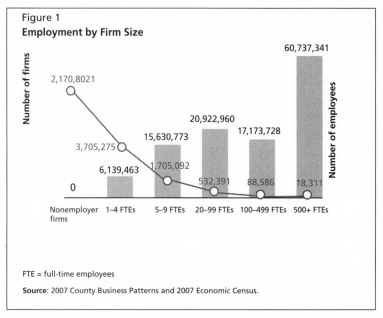

Figure 1
Employment by Firm Size

FTE = full-time employees
**Source**: 2007 County Business Patterns and 2007 Economic Census.

and contribute to "job churn"—that all-too-cyclical phenomenon in the workforce where our economy sheds jobs as quickly as it creates them. And the evidence shows that what really creates jobs that last is investing in *mature* businesses—firms whose management has found ways to keep them afloat—if not thriving—for over twenty-five years.[4] That point is profoundly unsexy, I know. But that doesn't make it any less true. It is equally true, though unpopular to state, that our nation doesn't need more entrepreneurs: we simply need better-prepared entrepreneurs.

What those of us who care about helping entrepreneurs must do is teach them not just how to start a business, but how to start a business that will be sustainable. It's sustainable businesses that help create broad value beyond the return to their own shareholders and consumer base and create good jobs that last beyond a quarterly job report from the Department of Labor, or longer than an election cycle.

We don't often dream about being a mom-and-pop outfit, but these small-scale, community-centered businesses are as key to the sustained vitality of our local economies as are the multinational corporations whose tentacles reach into virtually every neighborhood across the fruited plain.

Many entrepreneurs who have a good attitude, a great idea, and a willingness to work diligently will build businesses that do not survive long. Most may never get beyond the incubation stage, and therefore never generate enough revenues to allow the founders to leave their day jobs, let alone hire employees. Of the millions of businesses that exist in the U.S., most do just that: exist. They neither expand nor contract; they stagnate.

Certainly, I recommend having and maintaining a constructive outlook based on reality. I daresay a good attitude, a great idea, and a willingness to work hard are important things to have, particularly if the entrepreneurial road you have taken is a lonely and a daunting one. That said, a good attitude has not been proven to cause business success. And when one's optimism is based on wishful thinking that denies the unavoidable negativity entrepreneurs must repeatedly confront, such "positivity" is not only of dubious value, it is noticeably absent from the top predictors of entrepreneurial viability, as is revealed in chapter 4.

Rosalene Glickman makes this point well in her counterintuitive but compelling argument in her book *Optimal Thinking*:

> Many positive thinkers believe that their dreams will be realized by a magical, divine process that is triggered by the intensity of their hopes, wishes, and faith. They approach life with a false sense of security, and are ill prepared for negative consequences. Their positive thinking is often no more than wishful thinking and can be extremely dangerous.
>
> [Instead] acknowledge and respect negativity as an authentic expression of reality. When we notice ourselves finding fault and worrying, we accept our negative viewpoints, seek to understand them, and immediately ask the most constructive questions in order to find the best solution.[5]

By understanding invisible capital, how it works, and how best to leverage it, we may very well have to accept the inherent negativity in a system that has produced and distributed it so unequally. However, we can choose to be "positive" and ignorant, or realistic and solutions oriented with regard to improving entrepreneurial opportunity for ourselves and others despite the very long odds detailed in this book.

Some research suggests that certain individuals pursuing different forms of entrepreneurship exhibit a particular personality trait that includes a strong "internal locus of control." In other words, some entrepreneurs believe that much of what positively impacts business outcomes for their new venture is well within their own power to influence. However, while there may be a significant link between entrepreneurs who think this way and their likelihood of starting a new venture, there appears to be no meaningful correlation between the prevalence of this attitude among start-ups and the ultimate viability of those start-ups.

Despite ample research debunking the singular value of mind-set on business viability, whole cottage industries have been created to contradict this evidence in order to better market "secrets to business success" supported by neither research nor reality. (This unsavory phenomenon will be explored in chapter 4 as well.)

In defiance of the long odds of success in business, every year roughly 2 million start-up ventures are founded in the U.S.— slightly fewer than the number of marriages. Generally, most marriages fare better than most businesses. And even in light of the sorry state of matrimony these days, marriages still last longer than businesses.

Those who have not prospered in business—or, as is the case for most would-be entrepreneurs, those who never fully made it out of the starting gate—are not necessarily the people who lacked the psychological resolve, the creativity, or the "sweat equity" (that is, the work hours invested in the venture). They are often the individuals who lacked what I have coined "invisible capital."

### What Is Invisible Capital?

If capital is that form of wealth that when exchanged for a specific purpose produces more wealth,[6] then invisible capital is the collection of largely intangible assets that improve the probability that your venture will grow and thrive.

Invisible capital is the toolkit of our skills, knowledge, language, networks, and experiences, along with the set of assets we were born with: our race and gender, our family's wealth and status, the type of community in which we were raised, and the education we had as children. Some of these assets are fixed—we cannot change who our parents are. Others are in our power to modify. What makes all of them "invisible" is that our society does not acknowledge that entrepreneurial opportunities—and thus entrepreneurial outcomes— are greatly influenced by these assets.

Some of the assets in our invisible capital portfolio are quantifiable, such as work experience and the concrete skills, knowledge, and relationships that come from that job history. For example, we know from the 2008 Kauffman Firm Survey that the businesses that lasted the longest—up to 12 percent longer than their counterparts— were the ones run by people who had started two to three prior businesses.[7]

Entrepreneurs who have worked in family-owned businesses have an even better chance of success. Those who have wealth or meaningful access to it—through family or other networks—have a leg up, as do those who have managed to obtain a college degree. Choice of industry matters, as do race and gender, though perhaps not in the way we might assume—being a man may prove a disadvantage if you want to start a day care center.

Jocelyn's parents run a laundry, where she helped out as a child. In college, she created a venture doing laundry for other students. After college, she worked at a bank. When a friend wanted help setting up a dog-grooming business, she asked Jocelyn to be a partner. Jocelyn invested her small savings and helped her friend get a bank loan. Once the business was launched, her friend bought out Jocelyn's share. With the money, Jocelyn decided to leave her banking job for good and pursue her real passion: flower design. She set up her own business, serving weddings, special events, and flower shops that needed expert advice. Her business now supports Jocelyn and an assistant.

Jocelyn had invisible capital. She was able to use her experience with the family business to set up her own laundry business in college. She then used her college degree to get a job in banking, which helped her learn more about getting loans and also allowed her to save up a little nest egg. She used her newfound knowledge of banking, and her nest egg, to help launch the dog-grooming business, and then used the money she made from that to launch her own successful business. Jocelyn worked hard, but she also had the advantage of invisible capital—some of which she inherited at birth and some of which she acquired through the choices she made. It didn't matter that Jocelyn didn't even know what invisible capital was or how it worked to her advantage.

Invisible capital is critical to entrepreneurial success. How many people are stopped in their pursuit of business success just because they have no idea how to apply for a loan? If no one in your family or in your circle of friends has ever applied for a business loan, you may not know that banks offer them, you may not know how to distinguish a good rate from a bad one, and you may not know how to create the kinds of financial statements bankers like to see. There is a whole set of tools that go into the toolkit of getting a bank loan that are readily available to some people—and absolutely invisible to others.

### Invisible Capital Shifts the Entrepreneurial Paradigm

It would be nice if all an entrepreneur needed to succeed were to get those missing tools. I'd love to be able to say, "Buy this book, and I will give you all the elements you need for success!" But this book is not about handing you the proverbial keys to the secret kingdom of entrepreneurial fabulousness. Instead, it's about changing our mind-set about entrepreneurship—and learning what makes entrepreneurs more (or less) viable in this often high-stakes pursuit.

It's a paradigm shift from making a shallow call for increased investment in entrepreneurs and innovation to calling for innovative investment in comprehensive entrepreneurial literacy, and for building a toolkit that fosters broad opportunity for sustainable entrepreneurship toward shared prosperity.

President John F. Kennedy didn't lay out a detailed plan for exactly how we should send a man to the moon and return him safely back to Earth. Instead, he simply but powerfully extolled the virtues of—and commitment to—doing it because it was well within our collective ability and would yield great results if done in an aggressive, highly collaborative, and timely fashion. In a speech made to a joint session of Congress on May 25, 1961, President Kennedy proclaimed:

I believe we possess all the resources and talents necessary. But the facts of the matter are that we have never made the national decisions or marshaled the national resources required for such leadership. We have never specified long-range goals on an urgent time schedule, or managed our resources and our time so as to insure their fulfillment.

Let it be clear, ... I am asking the Congress and the country to accept a firm commitment to a new course of action, a course which will last for many years and carry very heavy costs. . . . If we are to go only halfway, or reduce our sights in the face of difficulty, in my judgment it would be better not to go at all.

... It is a most important decision that we make as a nation.

This decision demands a major national commitment of scientific and technical manpower ..., and the possibility of their diversion from other important activities where they are already thinly spread. It means a degree of dedication, organization and discipline which have not always characterized our research and development efforts.

... New objectives and new money cannot solve these problems. They could, in fact, aggravate them further—unless every scientist, every engineer, every serviceman, every technician, contractor, and civil servant gives his personal pledge that this nation will move forward, with the full speed of freedom, in the exciting adventure of space.[8]

Until that moment, most Americans believed that the stars were the realm of heaven, not of humankind. JFK changed all of that with this one bold and visionary speech to a restless nation desperately wanting to spread its wings and fulfill its promise in a fast-changing world. Kennedy's vision in pursuit of space travel was a paradigm shift of the highest order. It was an otherworldly goal for which we had little point of reference. A half-century later, we have not yet committed to taking such a bold step in a far more earthly and seemingly familiar endeavor of no less consequence than extraterrestrial exploration: entrepreneurship.

We are mired in an ignorance cloaked in a confident, yet unhealthy, view of material success that with each passing generation betrays any collective notion of equality of opportunity, social equity, and shared prosperity—at a time when our most vulnerable communities are in greatest crisis and our middle class is shrinking and increasingly beleaguered. In fact, according to Brandeis University's Institute on Assets and Social Policy (IASP), the wealth gap between White Americans and African Americans more than quadrupled in the twenty-three years from 1984 to 2007.[9]

According to acclaimed wealth guru Edward Wolff,

Most people think of family income as a measure of well-being, but family wealth is also a source of well-being, independent of the direct income it provides. There are both narrowly economic and broader reasons for the importance of wealth. Some assets, particularly owner-occupied housing, provide services directly to the owner. This is also true for consumer durables, such as auto-

mobiles. Such assets can substitute for financial income in satisfying economic needs.

... More important, perhaps, than its role as a source of income
is the security that wealth brings to its owners, who know that their
consumption can be sustained even if income fluctuates. Most assets can be sold for cash or used as collateral for loans, thus providing
for unanticipated consumption needs. In times of economic stress,
occasioned by such crises as unemployment, sickness, or family
breakup, wealth is an important cushion. The very knowledge that
wealth is at hand is a source of comfort for many families.[10]

This book seeks to raise the value of increased knowledge and
insight around the modern entrepreneurial landscape and the forces
that shape it. It is as much about addressing the cultural phenomenon
of American entrepreneurship as it is a primer for how to improve
one's viability in this perplexing and complex endeavor. While this
book can help new and prospective entrepreneurs, its value extends
far beyond practitioners to engage the far larger audience of supporters and advocates of entrepreneurship who see in its pursuit economic and social opportunities they themselves may never create, yet
are no less stakeholders in helping facilitate.

Many of the things that can build our invisible capital are neither
surprising nor unattainable. In fact, some of the things you may read
about here are efforts you have already made (or suggested to others)
without previously understanding the specific dynamics of invisible
capital as it influences entrepreneurial viability.

In certain circumstances, we can help entrepreneurs gain skills and
knowledge they did not have before. Would-be entrepreneurs can be
taught to know what EBITDA stands for,[11] how to dress to meet with
a loan officer, and how to act at a cocktail party. You can pursue more
formal training, increase your digital literacy, and seek out mentors
who already are in the field you aspire to join. In this book, I discuss
some of the skills that can be taught and which resources can be ac-

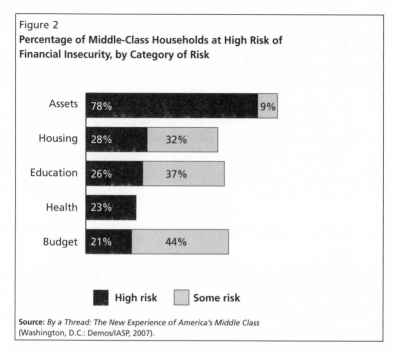

Figure 2
**Percentage of Middle-Class Households at High Risk of Financial Insecurity, by Category of Risk**

| | High risk | Some risk |
|---|---|---|
| Assets | 78% | 9% |
| Housing | 28% | 32% |
| Education | 26% | 37% |
| Health | 23% | |
| Budget | 21% | 44% |

**■ High risk    □ Some risk**

Source: *By a Thread: The New Experience of America's Middle Class*
(Washington, D.C.: Demos/IASP, 2007).

cessed. I talk about how you can identify what knowledge you lack and how you can build your personal networks.

However, there are sets of assets that cannot be acquired—we cannot change our race or gender, our native language, our families, or the communities in which we were raised. Nor should we. Certainly, whiteness and maleness are undeniable assets in our culture—and that's one reason that only about 29 percent of all businesses are female owned, and that Blacks and Latinos own roughly 7 percent and 8 percent of all businesses, respectively.[12] And it remains the case that there are male-oriented and female-oriented business pursuits (auto repair versus day care, say). However, invisible capital is not just a proxy for racism, sexism, classism, or heterosexism despite their enduring impact on our society, our democracy, and our economy.

People who are on the receiving end of these "isms" are not powerless, nor are they devoid of invisible capital. The playing field is not level, but each of us can do something to help level it, using the toolkit of our own skills, knowledge, networks, and experiences.

## Invisible Capital: A Zero-Sum Game

Invisible capital is a zero-sum game. We can "zero" out the unearned advantages others have by understanding what advantages we ourselves possess. We can learn to play the cards we have been dealt—whether we are White, Latina, or Chinese American, male or female—to develop our own entrepreneurial opportunities. We can level the playing field as entrepreneurs when we understand that invisible capital exists, when we learn what kinds of invisible capital we already have, and when we discover how to use it.

Assuming that you did not grow up in a bubble, you have a network of connections, a family or community that knows you, a set of experiences and skills you bring to the table. You may have a personal connection who would prove critical to setting up your business—but if you don't know how to network, if you don't understand what that person could offer, you can't take advantage of the connection. Understanding what you have—and what you lack—is the key to entrepreneurial opportunity and entrepreneurial success.

## Invisible Capital Creates Entrepreneurial Opportunity

Entrepreneurs who succeed leverage invisible capital to create opportunity. Every business, no matter how small, relies on a set of stakeholders who supply start-up capital, skills, and knowledge. Businesses that survive more than five years are not built by just one person, but by a team of people.

Entrepreneurs tend to bring into their projects people who look like themselves, have the same class status, and have the same type of invisible capital. If you happen to be a high-status, wealthy, college-educated man who has experience in a family business, your tendency to bring others like you to your team will probably be an asset. You have the kind of invisible capital that will instantly create opportunities for you.

Edward comes from a well-to-do family. His parents are doctors, but his uncle runs a small manufacturing business where Edward worked every summer. Edward went to the University of Illinois at Urbana-Champaign, where he joined a fraternity. After he graduated with a degree in mechanical engineering, he developed a new type of refrigerator latch. His uncle helped him manufacture a sample part, and he was able to raise $500,000 in start-up funds from his frat buddies. Edward's business was positioned to take off.

Edward did not need to understand his invisible capital—for him, the invisibility of his capital made his trajectory seem effortless. When Edward needed to take the next step on his entrepreneurial journey, opportunities appeared. Most people who want to manufacture a part would have a very hard time even figuring out whom to call first. Most people who need to raise $500,000 would not be able to raise that money by making fifteen phone calls. That is what I mean by the playing field not being level.

Disparate outcomes often suggest disparate opportunities.

Carlos comes from a poor family. His first language was Spanish, and his education was poor. He basically had to teach himself English by watching English-language TV. He worked his way through two years of community college, took two years off to work at Radio Shack to save up some money, then was able to get a BA in electrical engineering at the state university. While working at Radio Shack Carlos got an idea for an extension cord that would work better with new digital devices. He has made a prototype himself, but he doesn't know what his next step would be. Now working as the quality control engineer at the local electric company, Carlos has decided to focus on paying off his debts. He never becomes an entrepreneur.

Carlos has far fewer opportunities than Edward. He has almost none of the invisible capital he needs for the kind of enterprise he imagines. What's more, Carlos does not know what he lacks. Feeling as if he has hit a brick wall, Carlos gives up on his dream.

Most of us are like Carlos. Our playing field is not level. There's an old axiom that says, "Luck is when preparation meets opportunity."

Some people come well prepared. The rest of us need to acquire the skills, knowledge, resources, and networks we will need to take advantage of the opportunities that come our way.

Not everyone has the willpower to be an entrepreneur. We know that. What we don't always recognize is that even if someone has the drive and the will to be an entrepreneur, their lack of invisible capital might prove an impossible barrier. Entrepreneurial success depends upon learning to leverage and develop invisible capital to create opportunity.

## Entrepreneurial Success Arises from Opportunity

As an entrepreneur myself, as the director of a business incubator, and as a new-venture advisor, I have had the pleasure of teaching entrepreneurs how to access their invisible capital and create opportunity.

Have the people I worked with achieved the American Dream? Have they been able to build companies with hundreds of employees, leaving themselves the leisure to cruise around the world? No. That's because, for 99 percent of entrepreneurs, the American Dream never comes true. It's more likely, in fact, that the American Dream has actually prevented many people from going into business because it sets the bar so intolerably high.

Millions of Americans dream about going into business, but most Americans, like Carlos, don't start up their enterprises. They don't incorporate, don't acquire a federal tax identification number, don't start generating income. They have an idea, they may even have enough invisible capital to develop that idea into an opportunity, but they can't imagine that they will be able to achieve multimillionaire success. I believe in dreaming big, but believing that the only measure of success is becoming Donald Trump is going to be a barrier to your personal success.

Even business schools don't use the Trump model of success. The traditional business school definition of business success is whether a company has revenue, makes a recurring profit, has a highly productive and growing workforce, and operates profitably long enough to satisfy its stockholders' financial interest (read: maximize shareholder value). For most business schools, success equals viability. More to the point, if your company can make enough money to stay in business and return a profit in sustainable fashion, it's a success.

Implicitly, our government's standard for business success skews toward growth over profits because growth is often a proxy for economic prosperity and often correlates highly with low unemployment. In other words, growth equals job creation. And jobs equal happy politicians. So, by this lower standard, new ventures can be deemed successful simply by the fact that they exist and are at least a nominal representation of economic growth. If they hire one or two employees—be they full-time or part-time workers (with or without employee benefits)—it's worthy of celebration.

Suppose you run a day care center that employs yourself and one child care worker, generates modest revenue, and lasts several years. Even if your venture has never made a profit, you've hit three of the four criteria used to measure narrowly defined success. If you run a small construction firm that employs five to ten part-time day laborers, brings in money, and makes a small profit, even if your company is just a year old and cash flow is tight, you are also well within the realm of "success."

Support a payroll of just two people, and you've already beaten the odds—since only one out of four businesses have paid employees (including the "owner").[13] Employ twenty workers and you've made it into that rarefied top 3 percent of businesses with payrolls![14]

Every entrepreneur wants to beat the odds and create a viable business. But the American Dream tells us that viability isn't enough—we also need to acquire wealth to be successful. The American Dream tells us that the odds we need to beat are not four to one (the number of businesses with employees), but four hundred to one (the number of businesses that create real wealth for their owners).

Are those the odds you want to book? Is that your idea of success? Any entrepreneur about to embark on what is going to be the hardest work they have ever done in their lives should first ask, How do I measure success? What does success mean for me?

## The Richest Success Centers on Community

As Bill McKibben frames it, the richness of community is founded on civic engagement deeply rooted in companionship. He writes:

> Increased companionship "yields more happiness in individualistic societies, where it is scarce, than in collectivist societies, where it is abundant." What this means is: ... if you live in a suburban American home, buying another coffeemaker adds very little to your quantity of happiness. ... But since you live two people to an acre, a new friend, a new connection, is a big deal indeed. We have a surplus of individualism and a deficit of companionship, and so the second becomes more valuable.
>
> ... The math of the various quality-of-life indexes is daunting, but the results are clear: in the rich world, ... "feelings about people contribute more to subjective well-being than feelings about money, whether spent or saved."[15]

Few expressions are more trite than "giving back to the community." Yet in the best of times and the worst of times, most of us want to give ourselves to—and in turn be accepted by—a community: something that transcends place and centers on shared values, resources, goals, and experiences.

Sure, we may desire fast cars or bigger houses, but the most exhaustive research shows that consumption beyond a certain point has no positive impact on one's quality of life (in rich nations, anyway).[16] I know you may be tempted to say, "Well, let me be the first to disprove that research by trying to pull it off myself!" But sociologists generally agree that one of the biggest contributors to happiness is one's connection to community.[17]

Mom-and-pop establishments are most often associated not only with small business but with community-based enterprise. But while "community" has a nice ring to it, the word—like "entrepreneurship"—has become an empty vessel that means whatever any of us want it to mean to suit our purposes at the time.

There's no better example of this, in the wake of the Great Recession and the public antipathy toward big banks, than the lobbyist-created term "community bank," which is a misleading term of art for virtually every bank in the United States that's not among the top nineteen largest financial institutions that Americans just happen to hate the most. So-called community banks are just banks that happen to be located in your community. But that doesn't make them inherently good (or significantly better) than those big banks whose brands are household names. Call them what you will: if a small, local bank treats you as shoddily as the big boys do, who really cares about its size or location? Or as the Southernism goes, "Kittens in the oven don't make 'em biscuits!"

Just as we must challenge our assumptions about success, it is no less important to do so about the language we use that may affirm faulty reasoning. When we use the term "family owned and operated," we feel this label conveys a wholesome sensibility. Most of the time this feeling may be warranted. However, some of the most predatory funeral homes are family owned and community based. It is more an indictment of the "deathcare industry" (as it is known by its practitioners and industry insiders and analysts) than it is about individual families. So, "community based" and "community centered" may overlap, but they are certainly not the same thing. As a positive example, Craigslist is both a community-based enterprise (whose community is virtual) and largely community centered. (It is also worth noting that this industry-changing, multimillion-dollar company employs fewer than fifty people.)

Am I suggesting, with all this discussion about community, that you have to "do good" to succeed? No. But if it's a genuine interest of yours and can be of strategic benefit to the enterprise, then community-centered entrepreneurship—a subset of what I call "commonwealth enterprise" in chapter 6—can be a viable economic path to a kind of success most business schools, economists, and public officials too often dismiss or unduly marginalize.

Community-centered enterprises highly overlap with and are outgrowths of social entrepreneurship, which Jeffrey Robinson defines as "a process that includes: the identification of a specific social problem and a specific solution (or set of solutions) to address it; the evaluation of the social impact, the business model and the sustainability of the venture; and the creation of a social mission-oriented for-profit or a business-oriented nonprofit entity that pursues the double (or triple) bottom line."[18]

Those more open-minded entrepreneurship boosters have of late been advocating what they call a "triple bottom line," or the "3 Ps," by which they mean that all businesses should measure success by how much profit they make, how many people they help, and how their business betters the planet. For example, an ice cream store owner would create a triple bottom line by making money on her ice cream (profit), offering employees a living wage and health benefits (people), and using only organic milk, potato starch spoons, and recyclable cups (planet).

I'm all in favor of businesses that can pull off the triple bottom line, but doing so is not necessarily the same as building commonwealth enterprises whose missions are inherently community centered. Triple-bottom-line businesses are rarely easy to set up and often expensive to operate. They often require entrepreneurs to be highly educated, especially about environmental issues; connected to suppliers who can supply organic and recyclable goods at reasonable prices; skilled at marketing to the small percentage of Americans who are willing to spend more for triple-bottom-line products; and be located or able to relocate in a community of such people. In short, entrepreneurs need a tremendous amount of a very specific type of invisible capital to pull off this kind of business.

An entrepreneur who wants to start an ice cream shop in an inner-city community to serve kids near the local high school may not be able to create a viable business if she tries to make her ice cream "ecologically correct" or tries to pay her employees significantly above the minimum wage. Her product may be too expensive for her intended customers to buy. Yet that ice cream shop owner is creating an immediate, direct benefit for her community. She's creating jobs for local youth; she's improving the area with a thriving business; she's probably creating a safe hangout spot for teens. Her homemade and affordable ice cream has broader impact than the fancy organic ice cream purveyed by the shop with the impressively small eco-footprint that employs people in a more economically stable neighborhood. And the inner-city shop has as its founding stakeholders the local school district, the PTA, the local community development corporation (CDC), and Small Business Development Center (SBDC), all invested in community in concrete ways that not only contribute to that local population, but may very well increase its chances of surviving and thriving.

There is a clear distinction to be made between doing a kind of good that leads to increased business viability and the more popular and no less easy task of doing good while doing well—though these two tasks are not necessarily independent of each other. Indeed, I'm advocating that entrepreneurs define success as building a viable, community-centered business, because being community centered is good for the entrepreneur as well as good for the community. Building a sustainable network within your own community increases your invisible capital while helping your community grow stronger.

## Why Invisible Capital Matters to All of Us

Good people with great vision, tenacity, and ingenuity can start businesses that never get off the ground. Millions, in fact. (I like to think that I've been among this large contingent once or twice.)

Too often, we see entrepreneurial stumblings as a sign of personal failings rather than the logical result of a lack of the right mix of resources (and a dose of good timing). Such resources are encapsulated in part by invisible capital, which takes into account those things that correlate to the increased preparedness and openness to opportunity that many believe are the key ingredients in luck. Without understanding which tacit assets a particular business requires, would-be entrepreneurs are bound to fail. The high price for this ignorance is paid not only by entrepreneurs themselves, but also by the households and communities that depend on those businesses' survival. More broadly, America as a whole suffers when each successive generation of entrepreneurs enters this maze without understanding the invisible barriers to their chances of long-term survival.

Understanding the role of invisible capital will enable more Americans to create new business ventures; build wealth; create more jobs; innovate new products, services, technologies, business methods, and processes; increase the tax base; and, ideally, bolster communities—from historic neighborhoods to new digital constituencies.

Invisibility masks and protects certain advantages that should not remain whether or not we know they exist. The conscious act of democratizing entrepreneurial opportunity will help dissolve these disparities, aid those at a disadvantage to flourish, and strengthen the social fabric of our society.

# 1

# Dreaming a Difficult Dream

This book was born out of passion, history, and, yes, failure (or so I thought at the time). After the one-two punch of the spring 2000 tech-stock slide and the September 11, 2001, attacks, my brother and I finally agreed to suspend operations of the technology-based product design firm we had launched five years prior. This venture had been dying a slow death in perennial start-up mode due to lack of working capital (among a host of other factors).

I thought I had entered that project with my eyes wide open. After all, I had worked on Capitol Hill dealing with business development and federal procurement issues. I had worked for a federal commission on entrepreneurship. I had been surrounded by and strongly influenced by entrepreneurs throughout my life—had even researched them as a genealogist in my own family tree. And I had built a small-scale, modestly profitable business when I was in college, selling T-shirts, hats, and such to my fellow collegians and eventually customers in various locales in Chicago and other markets along the Eastern Seaboard.

Like most entrepreneurs, I had ignored the statistics and assumed that I would be the one to defy the odds. What I didn't realize then is that the deck was stacked against me despite the various traits and resources I brought to the table. In fact, they just were not enough. I didn't understand what the odds were, or how to play them. I read innumerable how-to books about business plans, but none of them taught me how to prepare for the rough-and-tumble entrepreneurial world.

## Running the Numbers

Based on statistics drawn from the most recent Kauffman Firm Survey, which followed nearly 5,000 U.S. start-up ventures from 2004 to 2008,[1] the odds of starting a business that lasts at least four years, generates revenues greater than $25,000, and goes on to hire at least one employee by its fourth year are about one in eight. To put these numbers in context, the average acceptance rate at an Ivy League college in 2009 was just under 16 percent.[2]

Generally speaking, as a nation, we encourage young folks (and not-so-young folks) to start their own businesses, but we rarely tell them *how* to prepare to become successful business owners—often implying or even declaring outright that you don't need a college education to thrive as an entrepreneur: "Look at Bill Gates; he was a college dropout!" But of those who hold up Bill Gates as an example, how many fill in the blanks? After all, Bill Gates dropped out of Harvard College, not MetroTech Community College. (He was also born rich.)

While Harvard was less selective in the 1970s than it is in the present era, it still was no cakewalk to get into—but it was much easier to get into and graduate from Harvard than to build the company that would become Microsoft. In fact, it's fair to say that it's probably vastly easier to get into Harvard than to build a business that will employ 20,000 people, 2,000 people, 200 people—or even 20 people, which happens to be the number of employees that the average "employer-firm" has on its payroll. In 2009, Harvard accepted only 7 percent of applicants into the Class of 2012. But fewer than 3 percent of all firms employ twenty or more people. (If any of these statistics surprise you, you now know why I wrote this book!)

Employer-firms, as the SBA calls them, are the one-fifth of all businesses that have a payroll—those that employ salaried or hourly workers. Of that one-fifth of firms with employees, almost 11 percent employ twenty or more people.[3]

In many respects, building a business is like entering a triathlon. Both pursuits seem very ambitious from the perspective of less adventurous souls—but they're not nearly as impressive as *growing* that business or actually *finishing* that race. It's fairly easy to sign up for a triathlon; the challenge, of course, is *doing* it—let alone being competitive in it!

Now, the likelihood of ascending to Bill Gates's stature in business and the likelihood of being accepted by and graduating from Harvard are two very different things. It's like comparing apples to oranges, or, as is the case with Gates, windows to doors. But whatever metaphor is most appropriate here, you get the point: starting a business that lasts and grows—let alone one that earns a consistent profit—is ridiculously hard.

If you've ever been asked to speak to a class of high schoolers, you probably know that you don't encourage students to apply to Harvard without knowing their scholastic aptitude. To do so would be reckless at best, and cruel at worst. Yet every day people tell folks to start a business based on little more than hearing someone's "great idea." Would you tell a senior in high school who has mediocre grades, no extracurriculars, and skipped taking the SAT to apply to Harvard just because she really, really wanted to go there?

When we encourage young people to go to college, it is because we know that doing so opens up more professional and other career opportunities and the likelihood of securing better-paying jobs. That's been the traditional thinking, anyway—certainly before the Great Recession. We also know that there are thousands of schools to choose from that can help students receive a good education, stimulate their intellectual development, expand their skills and life experiences, and improve their chances of joining the workforce after graduation. Few people claim that setting your sights on an elite, highly selective college is the *only* way to obtain an excellent education and good prospects of economic uplift. Yet when we tell people

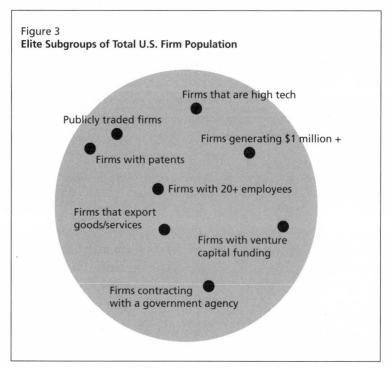

Figure 3
**Elite Subgroups of Total U.S. Firm Population**

Firms that are high tech

Publicly traded firms

Firms generating $1 million +

Firms with patents

Firms with 20+ employees

Firms that export
goods/services

Firms with venture
capital funding

Firms contracting
with a government agency

that they should go into business for themselves, particularly starting a company that will eventually require employees, we are essentially saying "Go to Harvard" to people whose scholastic track record may not be that competitive.

Why do we do it? Because we don't know any better. But I suspect when you're done reading this book, you'll resist the urge to tell someone who likes eating cake to open up his own bakery.

The good news is that in the United States, starting a business is pretty darn easy. All you have to do is figure out what you want to do, come up with a catchy name, print out a bunch of business cards on your printer, and get a business license at city hall, and you're technically in business. And if you report even the pittance you may have made in the previous tax year, the IRS will label your activity—whether it's babysitting or getting paid to speak at an event—as a business enterprise that must file a Schedule C, the tax form that documents the nonemployee income and expenses of sole proprietorships, entities totaling over 21 million in 2007.[4] Of course, this means that of the millions of firms that the IRS—and as a consequence, the U.S. Census Bureau—recognizes as businesses, only a fraction actually consider themselves "in business," which explains in part why their enterprises' annual earnings represent on average less than 10 percent of the revenues of their counterparts with payrolls.[5]

But what if you want to start the next Netflix or Cold Stone Creamery? What if you want to start a business that will grow to hundreds (or thousands) of employees in a nice office building—the kind of business that will net you enough take-home pay to retire to a life of leisure?

People planning to start new businesses often imagine that their businesses will grow big enough to employ hundreds of workers simply because most of us work at those kinds of large companies. Firms with over 2,500 employees account for 64 percent of the American workforce, even though they make up less than 1 percent of all U.S. firms.[6]

Let's sum up. Three out of four businesses have no employees. Nine out of ten employer-firms have fewer than twenty employees. So just getting to the point where you have done well enough to hire a few people is a nontrivial feat—only about 2 in 100 companies make it to that point. Hiring employees is not usually a business owner's first concern, however. Their first concern is usually *staying* in business one way or another.

No one wants to run a business that just barely makes ends meet, whether or not it has employees. Entrepreneurs start businesses to make a profit—even tree-hugging, Birkenstock-wearing entrepreneurs. And just as a highly relevant point of reference, the average business without employees brings in just over $45,000 a year.[7] (Given how many hours that business owner's probably working to make this amount, his hourly wage would make a low-paying, semiskilled job look pretty appealing!) Of course, staying in business is a reasonable concern and a necessary goal. But there's a big difference between surviving in business and thriving in business. It's the difference between wanting not to die and choosing to live well.

For some entrepreneurs, though, the dream is not to just "make it," but to "make it big," which for many entrepreneurial aspirants means building a highly scalable business. This higher threshold therefore requires that the dreamer's business not only generate recurring profits, but generate enough operating cash flow for the business owner to retain the funds (personally) to buy that vacation villa in the Caribbean, that Italian sports car, and an exclusive country club membership.

Remember: according to the Kauffman Firm Survey, only about 13 out of every 100 newly minted business owners surveyed survived four years, made over $25,000 in annual revenues, and hired employees. Surely, these milestones are nothing to sneeze at, but they are far from what is necessary to buy that Ferrari or oceanfront property in Antigua.

According to the Kauffman Foundation's *Anatomy of an Entrepreneur* study, the average entrepreneur is a White, middle-aged, well-educated man with a wife and kids and considerable experience in the industry in which he established his new venture.[8] Does this sound like you? Odds are it doesn't.

So what does this average entrepreneur have to do with you? Nothing—unless you want to know how close to average you are in terms of the probability you will establish a viable business. After all, if the example presented in the previous paragraph represents conventional business success (on a fairly modest scale), it's a fair question to pose whether you are more or less likely to achieve this success than "the average guy."

How do we arrive at averages, anyway? Simply put, in order to find an average (or what in statistics is called the *mean*), we add the sum of the total numbers and divide by the amount of those numbers we've added up. So let's assign the value zero to represent an average person's chances of being among the 12 out of every 100 new business owners who go on to modest success. Of course, some people

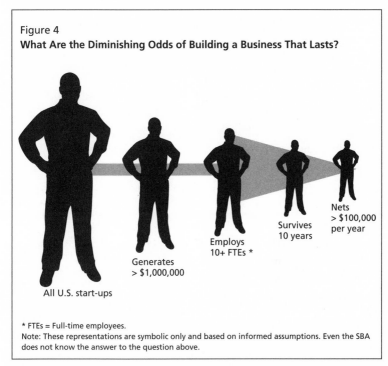

Figure 4
**What Are the Diminishing Odds of Building a Business That Lasts?**

Nets
> $100,000
per year

Survives
10 years

Employs
10+ FTEs *

Generates
> $1,000,000

All U.S. start-ups

\* FTEs = Full-time employees.
Note: These representations are symbolic only and based on informed assumptions. Even the SBA does not know the answer to the question above.

are going to be in a better-than-average position to achieve success; we can represent their chances by assigning them values above zero. Others may be ill equipped to survive, and we can represent their chances with values below zero.

For example, we could rate two entrepreneurs at –2 and two at +2. The average—or the mean—for these four enterprising souls would equal zero. So, too, would four individuals rated –50 and +50, –75 and +75. But, as shown in Figure 4, just as likely would be four people rated –79, +92, +8, and –21. In this scenario, which number best represents you? If you're modest, you might surmise you're at +8, if par is zero. But how would you know for sure? Could you really be –21? Or even worse, that dismal –79?

But the statistics tell a more sobering story, which means that some large percentage of new entrepreneurs are not just overly optimistic, they're absolutely clueless, and thus inordinately ill-prepared for their journey. They *literally* don't have a clue because few people in the average entrepreneur's sphere are in a position to alert them to the unseen forces that shape entrepreneurial opportunity—in particular, those things that will significantly boost their chances of achieving even modest success in business.

Not breaking out the champagne, are you? For good reason. Running a viable business that lasts is not for the faint of heart or the easily dissuaded. Running one that generates serious wealth for its owner is highly unlikely when you give the aforementioned statistics some serious thought. Granted, you have a better chance of succeeding in business than of winning the Powerball jackpot, but playing the lottery is much less work (and a lot less taxing on your bank account, your credit card balances, your personal relationships, and your stomach lining).

### Unknowns Worth Knowing

In a country so obsessed with starting up one's own business, inventing, pioneering, and becoming one's own boss, you might imagine that we know quite a bit about the landscape of modern American enterprise.

We don't.

In fact, generally speaking, Americans are entrepreneurial illiterates. We know very little about the inputs, outputs, and outcomes related to our vibrant entrepreneurial sector. We don't know much about its composition, productivity, or impact, let alone its history. This sad reality is not a consequence of low intelligence, however, just sparse knowledge. We think we are well informed because we watch a lot of television. We also know a lot of people who have started businesses (or at least are always talking about starting one). And, of course, we patronize innumerable businesses in our neighborhoods, near where we work, wherever we travel, and wherever we surf online.

Wordsmith extraordinaire Donald Rumsfeld, President George W. Bush's first secretary of defense, offered as clear a statement as I've

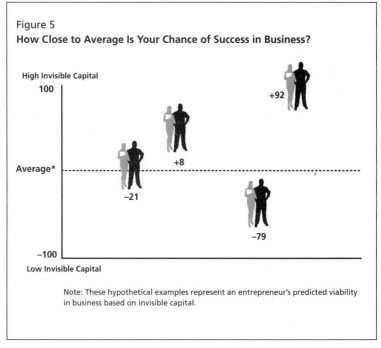

Figure 5
How Close to Average Is Your Chance of Success in Business?

High Invisible Capital
100

+92

Average*

+8

−21

−79

−100

Low Invisible Capital

Note: These hypothetical examples represent an entrepreneur's predicted viability in business based on invisible capital.

found on the state of entrepreneurship (he was, of course, talking about the state of the war in Iraq):

> Reports that say that something hasn't happened are always interesting to me, because as we know, there are *known* knowns; there are things we *know* we know. We also know there are known *unknowns*; that is to say, we *know* there are some things we do not know. But there are also *unknown* unknowns—the ones we don't *know* we don't know. And if one looks throughout the history of our country and other free countries, it is the latter category that tends to be the difficult ones.[9]

We think we know, generally, what entrepreneurship is. We may realize we don't know *everything* about starting our own enterprise. But there is a whole host of significant facts about entrepreneurship that we don't even know that we don't know.

How are most new businesses started? Almost half of all new enterprises were seeded with their founders' personal funds. Fewer than 4 percent of start-ups run by family members raise money from friends. Related co-founders of new ventures are 15 times less likely to raise funds from friends than are their nonfamily counterparts. Yet about 80 percent of all U.S. businesses are family owned. Roughly half of all new businesses are started out of their founders' homes.

On a related note, firms started by business owners who have run two or three previous businesses have higher survival rates than those started by first-timers.[10] Most family-owned businesses rarely survive past the second generation of owners. Venture capital–backed firms accounted for 11 percent—or about 12 million—of the 115 million private sector jobs in 2008.[11]

Perhaps the single most useful fact for politicians during economic downturns and campaign seasons is that firms operating for over twenty-five years, irrespective of size, create more net jobs than new firms. In fact, according to the U.S. Department of Labor, no category of younger firms creates net jobs.[12] This single, woefully underreported fact suggests that the *real* engine of sustained economic growth is U.S. firms that have mature, time-tested management and long track records—firms that may also be entrepreneurial even though they are not necessarily young or small-scale ventures. Too often, politicians and uncritical entrepreneurship boosters purposely or unintentionally equate "small businesses" with entrepreneurial ventures, innovation with advanced technology, new with better, and family owned with small.

The truth of the matter is that entrepreneurship is a *process*—a way of thinking—more than a firm's size, age, industry, or organizational setup. Apple Inc. is the world's highest-valued publicly traded technology company, recently outpacing Microsoft—and, arguably, a highly entrepreneurial entity, despite having over 17,000 employees. Ford Motor Company is family owned in that the Ford family still owns about a 40 percent stake in the business and until recently the company was run by a descendant of the founder. So too are

Motorola, Rupert Murdoch's News Corp., Johnson & Johnson, Walmart, and Tyson Foods—none of which can be mistaken for small on any level.[13] General Electric prides itself on innovation, yet it is no spring chicken, having been founded by the iconic American inventor Thomas Alva Edison in 1890.

What we learn from these facts—besides understanding just how difficult it is to build a business—is that it's a good idea to ask what kinds of businesses are most viable and how they got started.

## Business in America: An Overview

As of 2007, there were nearly 30 million documented businesses in the United States.[14] Firms with paid employees accounted for 5.5 million of all U.S.-based businesses. Sectors that were overrepresented among these businesses included construction; professional, scientific, and technical services; health care and social assistance; and other uncategorized services. Together, the firms within these four sectors represented nearly half of all the businesses the U.S. Census lists as part of the nation's economy. Interestingly, businesses with 500 or more employees within these four sectors combined account for less than 2 percent of all such firms.

Over half of U.S. firms are home based: 58 percent of nonemployer businesses are home based versus 22 percent of businesses with paid employees. There is a noticeable correlation between business revenues and being home based. Nearly 65 percent of businesses making less than $5,000 are home based compared to less than 6 percent of firms with revenues of $1 million or more. Not surprisingly, the data show that as business workforce size increases, the likelihood of having a home base drastically decreases: the largest percentage of employer-firms that are home based, at 29 percent, are businesses with 1–4 employees.

Those who hang out a shingle to leverage their own skills, expertise, and experience often represent what are commonly referred to as the self-employed. These individuals may prefer "being their own boss," despise bureaucracy, or seek greater flexibility to honor that nebulous equilibrium known as "work–life balance." Some subset of the self-employed are professionals such as lawyers, accountants, and consultants, people who often do not plan to grow their businesses in terms of hiring employees or becoming a highly scalable enterprise.

The self-employed who operate in the service economy by leveraging their skills, credentials, experiences, and networks—their invisible capital—are also known as independent knowledge workers or "entreprofessionals." Even though they are not necessarily innovating in their business, they may be taking career risks by choosing to end their search for employment, as noted in a recent *New York Times* op-ed piece by former Clinton-era secretary of labor Robert Reich. Reich alluded to the fact that in the span of just three years, from 2001 to 2003, the number of individuals who pursued self-employment by forming subchapter S corporations ("S-corps") and limited liability companies (LLCs) increased by over 12 percent. Appropriately, his column was entitled "Entrepreneur or Unemployed?"[15]

The self-employed also include business owners who are franchisees or multilevel marketing associates. Franchisees are individuals (or groups of individuals) who essentially buy a business model in a box. Based on a 2002 U.S. Census Bureau survey of business owners, they represent fewer than 4 percent of all firms with employees.[16] Running a franchise is neither cheap nor easy to do well. In fact, despite the seemingly obvious advantages of buying into an already market-tested business, some research shows that the odds of success in franchising may be lower than for business owners who create their enterprises from scratch.[17]

Even so, franchise survival rates are surely higher than those for multilevel marketing (MLM) businesses—enterprises also known as *network marketing organizations* or *direct sales organizations*, including well-known companies such as Mary Kay, Avon, and Amway. MLMs have earned a poor reputation for having an unethical business model, some being little more than pyramid or Ponzi schemes. That said, according to the Direct Selling Association website, over 15 million

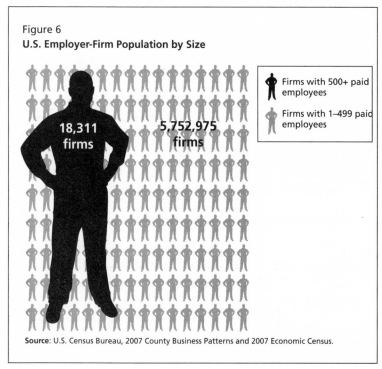

Figure 6
U.S. Employer-Firm Population by Size

18,311 firms

5,752,975 firms

Firms with 500+ paid employees

Firms with 1–499 paid employees

Source: U.S. Census Bureau, 2007 County Business Patterns and 2007 Economic Census.

people are involved in direct selling, reaching 74 percent of all Americans and accounting for over $114 billion in sales worldwide.[18]

Indeed, there exist at least a few socially conscious multilevel marketing companies,[19] just as there exist highly unscrupulous nonprofit organizations. Ultimately, though, an enterprise's business model will shed the most light on its organizational values. The MLMs that profit by design from their members' failure to sell mediocre (or worse) products or services after they have bought an expensive initiation fee are sadly the norm, with only a few notable exceptions. An MLM's products and services are rarely what generates the most profits for it; that would instead be the initial fees that systematically provide the continuous infusion of cash extracted from each successive wave of often underemployed, unemployed, retired, or otherwise cash-strapped new sales associates (also known in the industry as "independent business owners").[20]

## It's a Family Affair

To most folks, the term "small business" is synonymous with the mom-and-pop businesses we have all patronized, worked in, talked about nostalgically with family members, or seen depicted on TV, in the movies, or in books. Eighty percent of U.S. firms are family owned and operated. Most are run as sole proprietorships that have no formal legal or business structure, while the largest are structured as private or publicly traded corporations.

We envision the corner store, the neighborhood diner, the barber shop, the dentist's office, or the auto repair shop. *These* are small businesses, not the ones closing in on 500 employees, right?

Even if the employment threshold for small businesses were drastically lowered to fewer than 100 employees, there would still only be about 2 percent of U.S. firms *not* categorized as "small." So we need not use the term "small businesses," since they are the rule and not the exception. We should really just say "businesses" and "big businesses." After all, we don't say, "I'm an under-seven-feet-tall person." We simply say, "I'm a person." Why? Because over 99 percent of people walking the planet are *significantly* shorter than seven feet tall! We call these exceptionally tall people "seven-footers." The point is, we compare these human skyscrapers to the majority of the population, not the other way around.

As a result, how we reframe size itself shifts not only what we consider to be "big," but what is realistically achievable for the average American. "Big" when it comes to business is indeed the exception, and we should lower the bar significantly, if only to better correlate our worldview with the actual business landscape and the likelihood of entrepreneurs growing ventures of scale.

## Still Want to Start a Business?

We're told that starting a business is the secret to financial success (if you watch infomercials and venture into your email account's bulging spam folder, anyway). We've also been told that variable-rate mortgages never go up and that credit card interest rates will stay low. Sure. *Some* people can make the numbers work, and their businesses grow. Most businesses, however, die on the vine.

The data reveal that most U.S. firms do not even sprout. Many folks may have great business ideas, but they don't plant the right seeds in the right season or in the proper soil. They don't acquire a federal tax identification number. They don't apply for a business license, or vendor permits. They don't build the right teams, let alone retain a lawyer, an accountant, or a bookkeeper. They don't dedicate enough time to the business (which explains the high correlation between the extremely low average gross revenues for U.S. firms and the number of firms that are essentially run as glorified hobbies). They don't start generating income, and as a practical result they do not and cannot hire employees. As the IRS likes to put it, the business owner "has not materially worked on the business."

Most businesses are sideline enterprises run by otherwise employed, unemployed, chronically underemployed, or retired individuals. The lion's share of these informal ventures will linger indefinitely or outright die. Only a small percentage of new ventures will experience steady or significant growth in terms of revenue.

The deck is stacked against most nascent entrepreneurs. Yet some folks beat the odds and prevail. Our task is to understand how and why entrepreneurship appears to be so much more viable a path for some, but not others.

In the meantime, though, let's have a moratorium on using the term "small business" until polls show that most Americans have learned the difference between what we generally perceive as small and how economists and our government actually define it.

# 2

# The Landscape of Modern American Enterprise

Would-be entrepreneurs and business owners abound in the United States. These prospective entrants to the business world come from different corners of the workforce and beyond; they are employed, underemployed, unemployed, self-employed, semiretired, and retired. The late U.S. Supreme Court Justice Potter Stewart once said when defining obscenity, "I know it when I see it." The same can be said of entrepreneurship.

You might think that in this entrepreneurship-crazy nation, we would know an entrepreneur when we see one. However, there's really no universally accepted definition of entrepreneurship. Definitions range from the high-minded to the pragmatic, from the whimsical to the unimaginative.

An entrepreneur can be defined simply as "anyone who starts a business." The fancier way of saying this can be found in Webster's dictionary, which defines an entrepreneur as anyone who engages in "the activity of organizing, managing, and assuming the risks of a business or enterprise." However, many of those who study entrepreneurs prefer the more specific definition that entrepreneurship evangelist and author Ray Smilor attributes to the Harvard Business School: "the pursuit of opportunity beyond the resources one controls."[1]

For those who shape public policy, entrepreneurs fill a very specific niche, starting businesses that are designed, as Peter Drucker states, to create new value. Drucker's long definition is worth highlighting here:

> In the United States, . . . the entrepreneur is often defined as one who starts his own, new and small business. . . . But not every new small business is entrepreneurial or represents entrepreneurship. The husband and wife who opened another delicatessen store or another Mexican restaurant in the American suburb surely take a risk. But are they entrepreneurs? All they do is what has been done many times before. They gamble on the increasing popularity of eating out in their area, but create neither a new satisfaction nor new consumer demand. Seen under this perspective they are surely not entrepreneurs even though there is a new venture . . . . Admittedly, all new small businesses have many factors in common. But to be entrepreneurial, an enterprise has to have special characteristics over and above being new and small.[2]

As I noted in the Introduction, according to a 2009 briefing issued by the U.S. Census Bureau's Business Dynamics Statistics, businesses over twenty-five years old are the only class of business that produces net job growth.

Drucker pointedly confirms that while the terms "entrepreneur" and "small business owner" are very often used as synonyms, they are not truly interchangeable. Most start-up ventures start small (and, by definition, are new), but not all (or even most) new ventures are in fact entrepreneurial. Entrepreneurship is much more a process and strategy than it is an organizational stage or an inborn disposition of the entrepreneur.

The two-dimensional assessment of entrepreneurship often paints it as a simple interaction between risk and reward, turning entrepreneurs into adrenaline-addicted caricatures in pursuit of the next great risk. The reality is that not all entrepreneurs are cut from the same proverbial piece of cloth. They are as diverse a group as any other, despite the tendency of our society to pigeonhole them as business daredevils. But it is not risk that is at the heart of entrepreneurship—instead, it's uncertainty.[3] If what characterizes risk is the prospect of danger, then ambiguity is the partner of uncertainty—sheer Kryptonite to those who require a clear and linear path toward professional fulfillment. And if comfort in living with uncertainty is indeed a common trait of "successful" or "serial" entrepreneurs, then perhaps it is this trait that is a proxy for the alleged "entrepreneur gene" that some researchers claim exists.

Whether you believe entrepreneurship is a genetic trait (or defect) or see it simply as reflecting a gambler's temperament, there are those like the late entrepreneur Victor Kiam who believe that "entrepreneurs are simply those who understand that there is little difference between obstacle and opportunity and are able to turn both to their advantage."

There is no better example of this than the "predators" that Malcolm Gladwell has described in *The New Yorker*.[4] In a fascinating essay titled "The Sure Thing: How Entrepreneurs Really Succeed," Gladwell illuminates the entrepreneur-as-predator by tracing the paths to great fortune of two businessmen, media mogul Ted Turner and Wall Street financier John Paulson. Gladwell's counterintuitive analysis undermines the very common notion that entrepreneurs are risk-takers, when in fact some of the most successful predators "seek to incur the least risk possible while hunting."[5] Gladwell contends that "the risk-taking model suggests that the entrepreneur's chief advantage is one of temperament—he's braver than the rest of us are. In the predator model, the entrepreneur's advantage is analytical—he's better at figuring out a sure thing than the rest of us."[6] What we will see in the next chapter is the hidden toolkit of invisible capital that such entrepreneurs possess to greatly facilitate their ability to decipher and access these sure things.

Both mountain lions and cheetahs are predators, but when their respective hunting grounds are swapped or significantly restricted, their learned and inborn abilities are heavily taxed. That tax in the business world is invisible capital—a tax that by virtue of its uneven effects hurts some and helps others. And while entrepreneurship must somehow relate to an ongoing economic activity, it is not inherently or solely related to profit-making. What determines whether an enterprise is entrepreneurial is the freshness of its products, services, processes, or structures, and whether the enterprise creates value for the consumer, market, or society itself. The people who make this kind of enterprise happen are entrepreneurs.

Conventionally successful entrepreneurs are those individuals who use opportunity like capital, by leveraging it to create even more opportunity to exploit for financial gain. As Gladwell points out, these folks are hardly gamblers—in fact, they're more like visionary accountants, calculating every transaction, process, and framework. Indeed, the entrepreneurs who are the biggest risk-takers are often the ones who need to be the most risk averse because they lack the insulation afforded by invisible capital.

The label "entrepreneurial gene" is misleading. It implies a biological predisposition to pursue or to prevail in business, when in fact it may only determine one's inclination toward the creative thinking and analysis at the heart of the type of innovation on which the richest form of entrepreneurship rests.

### Entrepreneurs Innovate

So what is the special sauce that makes some business owners entrepreneurs and others simply merchants? Innovation and opportunity. Opportunity is their muse, and innovation is their most favored tool. Innovation, Drucker tells us, "is the specific instrument of entrepreneurship." Because innovation is the key to entrepreneurship, we often imagine an entrepreneur as an inventor. For decades the media loved to tell the story of the lone engineer who invented the next technological advance in his garage and then built a business around it into a multimillion-dollar company. Can anyone say Apple?

From Ben Franklin to Thomas Edison to direct-response marketing pioneer Ron Popeil (the infomercial guru who coined the catchphrase "But wait, there's more!"), generations of inventors have continually earned our praise, admiration, and collective envy. Most inventors, however, are not entrepreneurs—even the rare ones who dutifully and painstakingly secure patents for their gizmos and gadgets.

Most inventors don't receive patents, and most inventors who do earn little more from their inventions than pride, ulcers, and invoices from their patent attorneys. What most people don't realize (inventors included) is that patents are not exclusive licenses to sell their inventions to the world; they are a means to keep others from doing so—and in theory more than in practice.

Having some direct experience with this, I will share with you what an intellectual property attorney sagely reminded me in his fancy downtown Chicago office many years ago: "Just because someone gets the patent for a nuclear-powered hovercraft doesn't give them the legal right to manufacture or sell it." It is also true that just because someone has been granted a patent doesn't mean that that asset will be honored by competitors or will have inherent or instant value in the marketplace. Most importantly, though, like a felled tree in the forest, if nobody of consequence knows you own the patent, is it worth the paper it's issued on or the considerable annual maintenance fees it incurs?

Also highly noteworthy is the fact that some of the most celebrated entrepreneurs we associate with groundbreaking inventions didn't invent them. Henry Ford did not invent the automobile. (He did, however, invent the term "horseless carriage.") Ford's revolutionary innovation was not the car but a more efficient process of making cars: assembly line production. The same can be said of Ray Kroc, who invented neither the hamburger nor french fries, nor the fast-food chain model itself. His genius was in *replicative* innovation, which all but perfected what we've come to know as fast food and the consistent taste, look, size, and experience that consumers can come to expect in any McDonald's anywhere in the world. Likewise, Bill Gates. Gates did not invent the personal computer (Steve Jobs did), nor did he develop the original operating system concept upon which Windows is based (Xerox did). Gates's genius was acquiring, refining, and licensing an operating system on which the vast majority of computers would eventually be run—starting with Microsoft's first licensee: IBM.

Innovation is not invention. Innovation is what economist Joseph Schumpeter called the "creative destruction" of our previous ways of thinking and organizing the economy. Ford changed how we thought about manufacturing; Kroc changed how we thought about a service industry; and Gates changed how we thought about office work. The biggest successes often come from innovations around process rather than product.

Perhaps because entrepreneurs are understood to engage in creative destruction, the conventional wisdom is that entrepreneurs are risk junkies, daredevils in suits, willing to pull everything apart before putting it back together. There is no credible evidence to support this common misperception. Various studies of entrepreneurial motivation have shown that there are both internal and external influences around new-venture creation on one axis and the degree of entrepreneurial intensity on the other.

The data reveal that those who pursue entrepreneurial activity are as diverse in personality, skill, and inclination as nonentrepreneurs. For instance, an entrepreneur can be a stay-at-home dad who sells handmade walking sticks via eBay as a "side hustle," and just as easily be a woman who has inherited her parents' demolition company and plans on making its stock available on the New York Stock Exchange (that is, "taking it public") within the next five years. There is no *one* kind of, or "true," entrepreneur.

Some entrepreneurs are growth oriented while others are passion oriented, the latter often correlating highly with what are known as "lifestyle" businesses—small-scale firms that are not built to become large in terms of payroll or revenues. Small office/home office (SOHO) ventures often exemplify lifestyle enterprises and significantly overlap with those firms that have no employees and many of the firms that have fewer than five or ten employees, also known as microenterprises. Some microenterprise owners are content with their firms' size, whereas a very small subset of microenterprises will mushroom in both employee count and sales.

Some researchers believe that chief among the variables contributing to success is entrepreneurial intensity, that self-described desire in some entrepreneurs to build a large-scale, highly profitable enterprise. As we will see in chapter 5, what some entrepreneurial researchers call "entrepreneurial intensity" is often what shapes our definition of success in terms of the number of people employed and the size of the profits returned.[7] However, the more we begin to understand invisible capital, the more readily we can see how even the earliest prelaunch choices people make are a direct consequence of what opportunities they feel they are capable of leveraging or even imagining.

Different people become entrepreneurs for different reasons. Some ventures are based on market opportunities. For others, necessity breeds entrepreneurial invention. As the joke goes, a reporter asked a newly minted business owner at what point she realized she was an entrepreneur. The woman replied, "I think it was something my last boss told me." The reporter asked what that was. She quipped, "'You're fired!'"

Some entrepreneurs aspire to obscene wealth, while others are inspired to make the world a better place. Some feel conditioned from birth to choose this way of life, while others are motivated by external factors such as prestige, greater flexibility, or more control over their lives. No doubt, the nature and complexity of these factors influence the various choices new entrepreneurs make as to how they build their ventures. So rather than being the wild-eyed, money-grubbing entrepreneurs are often characterized as, many are simply opportunists—in the best sense of that word. They either exploit or create opportunities others can't see or simply won't pursue.

## The Entrepreneur as Opportunist

America has often been called the Land of Opportunity. We believe in the rags-to-riches story popularized by the nineteenth-century novelist Horatio Alger Jr. In Alger's stories, the opportunity to rise from poverty to wealth is always there, waiting for a young man with the will and drive to succeed. But Alger did not come up with this story on his own. His story comes out of the Puritans' stoic work ethic, which Max Weber immortalized in his seminal book *The Protestant Ethic and Capitalism.*[8] The Puritans believed that hard work would lead to heavenly reward. In America, however, those rewards would also be material. Weber argued that the Puritan's drive to work was so strong that it basically led to the creation of an entrepreneurial economy. That is, not content with the usual 9-to-5 shift (or in the case of the earliest colonists, who were mostly farmers, the 6-to-4), early Americans sought out autonomy and innovation. They chose to abandon what was safe and secure for what was riskier but potentially more rewarding.

Other economists take a different view of Americans' entrepreneurial bent. They argue that the American economy required risk-taking and innovation, which led to the development of early entrepreneurs. Certainly, European settlers looked past, over, and through the native populations they found and saw a whole continent free for the taking.[9] They developed a belief in Manifest Destiny, the view that Euro-Americans were destined to take this land to enrich themselves—that the American continent was an opportunity stretching from the redwood forest to the Gulf Stream waters, in folksinger Pete Seeger's phrase. Patriotism was defined as taking the initiative to conquer the land. Early stories celebrated figures like Daniel Boone, who uprooted his family over and over again to take a risk on the frontier.

What all the historians agree upon is that we Americans truly believe we live in a land of opportunity where hard work, determination, and risk-taking will bring material rewards. From America's most beloved founding father, Benjamin Franklin, to "positive thinker" Norman Vincent Peale, Americans have defined ourselves as a people who believe that we can "be all that we can be" if we are self-determined and industrious. Understandably, these ideas have molded the manner in which many of us see entrepreneurship. In the Land of Opportunity, we view entrepreneurship through the lens of virtuous possibility and not through the much clearer window of entrepreneurial probability.

For over a hundred years, America did provide unusual opportunities for its newest settlers. From the 1600s to the 1800s, risk-takers prospered by driving Native Americans off their land and converting that land to agricultural use. The 1800s brought the Industrial Revolution to the United States, and with it a wave of entrepreneurship that irrevocably changed the very nature and impact of American business. That new industrial economy was boosted into the stratosphere in the 1940s by World War II. The only industrialized nation whose infrastructure was not destroyed by the war, the United States became the engine for the world's economy.

The wealth, prosperity, and upward social and economic mobility created by the New Deal, the war, and legislation like the GI Bill, coupled with the expansion of affordable housing and consumer goods, made the American Dream seem real and attainable to millions. It is within this postwar context that modern American entrepreneurship emerged.

### Whose Opportunity?

Studies show that Americans are the world's most productive workers. According to a 2007 United Nations report, "The average US worker produces $63,885 of wealth per year, more than their counterparts in all other countries. ... Ireland comes in second at $55,986, followed by Luxembourg at $55,641, Belgium at $55,235, and France at $54,609."[10]

If the Puritans were right, then hard work should lead to big rewards. Yet we also know that a majority of hardworking Americans who start their own businesses see those businesses close within the first few years of starting up. Clearly, there are opportunities out there for some American entrepreneurs. The question is, which ones, and why?

## Who Are America's Entrepreneurs?

America's entrepreneurs are women and men of every social class and ethnicity, from megalopolis and hamlet, across the great breadth of this nation. However, people with some backgrounds are more likely to be entrepreneurs than others. Though women represent a slight majority in terms of the overall population, according to a longitudinal study conducted by the Kauffman Foundation, fewer than 28 percent of all U.S. firms are female owned.[11]

People born in the United States account for about 90 percent of business owners in the U.S.; only 7 percent of business owners are naturalized citizens or documented residents. The ranks of the entrepreneurial class are also woefully underrepresented as far as African Americans and Latinos are concerned: Black people make up roughly 13 percent of the U.S. population, yet account for only 7.1 percent of

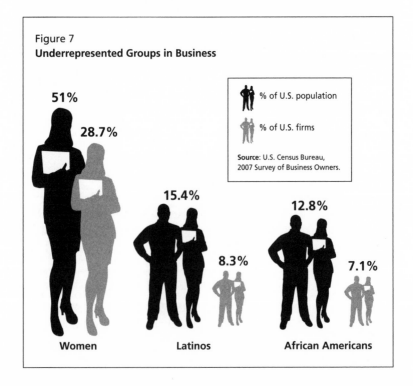

Figure 7
**Underrepresented Groups in Business**

51%
28.7%

👥 % of U.S. population

👥 % of U.S. firms

Source: U.S. Census Bureau, 2007 Survey of Business Owners.

15.4%
12.8%
8.3%
7.1%

Women          Latinos          African Americans

all business owners; Latinos total about 15 percent, but represent just 6.8 percent of all business owners.[12]

Of course, if some people are less inclined to start businesses than others, these numbers might make sense. However, in actuality, these numbers portray the complexity of this issue. For instance, even though African Americans are underrepresented in business ownership and show significantly lower employee counts and gross receipts per firm, they are actually the demographic group in our nation most likely to start businesses—not White men or newly immigrated Americans, as indicated in Figure 8. Clearly, how invisible capital influences entrepreneurial opportunity is negatively impacting a portion of would-be and nascent business owners between the time they set out to start a new venture and its actual operation in the marketplace.

Figure 8
**Black Men and Women Are 50% More Likely Than the Average American to Start a Business**

*(Between ages 25-44)*
Black Americans
All Americans

15.9%
10.6%
9.9%
6.6%

Source: *The Entrepreneur Next Door: Characteristics of Individuals Starting Companies in America* (Kansas City, Mo.: Kauffman Foundation, 2002), 5.

Business owners tend to be well educated. Over 64 percent of business owners had at least some college education at the time they started or acquired their businesses—a percentage that is noticeably higher than the proportion of the general adult population with the same educational attainment (52 percent).[13] Of those with college credits, 23 percent had a bachelor's degree, and 17 percent had earned an advanced degree. A striking 56 percent of business owners of firms with employees held graduate degrees, while 72 percent of majority-interest owners of nonemployer firms were similarly educated.

You might think that all entrepreneurs at least are motivated by the desire to maximize profits—or, in effect, by greed. Well, you'd be wrong. Entrepreneurs are as diverse as any other group of people. Some entrepreneurs are born out of necessity. There are entrepreneurs who create new ventures because they invented something they (and perhaps only they) think is revolutionary, and there are others who are refugees from the service economy—knowledge workers—who have sought self-employment because they want more autonomy in their life or were involuntarily given more autonomy than they bargained for by being fired or laid off. The latter phenomenon is wrenchingly chronicled in Barbara Ehrenreich's book *Bait and Switch: The (Futile) Pursuit of the American Dream*.

The entrepreneurial profile—and the pathways to business creation itself—are as diverse as the landscape and people of America. So, too, are the types of firms created, the industries they operate in, and how they are financed, structured, managed, and grown. And how these enterprises fare has much more to do with the inequities compounded by the uneven distribution of invisible capital than with the sunniness of any given entrepreneur's disposition.

## The Playing Field Is Not Level

Disparate outcomes often (though not always) suggest disparate opportunities. What the data above show is that the playing field is not level. Those who have built businesses before, those who have worked in a family business, and those who are college educated have

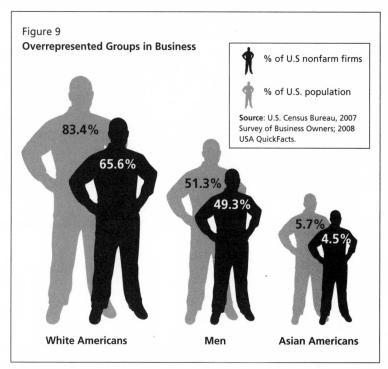

Figure 9
**Overrepresented Groups in Business**

% of U.S nonfarm firms

% of U.S. population

**Source:** U.S. Census Bureau, 2007 Survey of Business Owners; 2008 USA QuickFacts.

83.4%

65.6%

51.3%

49.3%

5.7%

4.5%

**White Americans**          **Men**          **Asian Americans**

an immediate advantage over those who haven't. There's truth in the axiom "Luck is when preparation meets opportunity." A playing field tilted to the advantaged few greatly impacts the quality of preparedness and range and depth of opportunity for those without significant tangible and intangible assets.

What all these statistics show us is that very few entrepreneurs are actually well prepared for the opportunities they meet. Their luck is bad because they aren't able to grab the opportunities that come their way. Why are they ill prepared? Is it a personal failing? For the most part, the answer is no. The best "preparation" for successful entrepreneurship turns out to mean, at least in part, being born into the right kind of family and the right kind of bodies and being placed in right kind of environment—these are factors that few of us can control. They are what I call "invisible capital."

# 3

# Invisible Capital Exposed

*Invisible capital is the wind. We don't see it, but it is undoubtedly there. Its presence is felt. Its impacts are clear, from the naked stalk of a dandelion to a felled grove of oceanfront palm trees.*

*For those striving to succeed in modern American entrepreneurship, invisible capital is either a powerful tailwind, a brutal headwind, or even a fickle, swirling windstorm, depending on your circumstances. For millennia, the wind was believed to be the breath of the gods. Anger them, and your village would be wiped out. Honor them, and the gods would spare you.*

*These days, most Americans are no more sophisticated when understanding the all-too-real, but unseen, forces that shape entrepreneurial opportunity. As Americans, we are like children who have neither fully processed nor correctly labeled a force of nature that we intuitively know exists but can't explain.*

*We watch with amazement when our kites ascend to the clouds and cry when they inexplicably crash to the ground. Some kites are constructed much better than others. Some of us are also much better kite flyers than others. But neither group has much chance of success when the wind doesn't blow.*

The United States may be the land of boundless opportunity, but that doesn't mean that it offers equality of opportunity. As we saw in chapter 2, you can predict which entrepreneurs will succeed with a fairly high degree of probability if you know some basic facts about them. And on the surface, race, gender, and the social class of their families seem like pretty obvious factors. It's simply easier for some people to succeed. The playing field is not level.

If you want to become an entrepreneur, or help other entrepreneurs succeed, you have to be able to level out that playing field. You have to understand the rules of the game. Those rules are not written anywhere. You can't find a referee to give you a rulebook—one has yet to be written with this landscape in mind by the very same institutions most vocal and influential regarding the cause of entrepreneurship. First you need to understand the lay of the land and navigate the often hidden obstacles on a playing field tipped in favor of those who already know the rules—or at least benefit from them the most. In fact, the rules are often not even well known or understood even by the "winners." That's because the rules of the game are largely invisible and sometimes the beneficiaries are unaware of the full range and impact of these unseen forces.

While it's hard for some people to imagine benefiting from things we don't consciously know exist, that's the story of the two fish. One fish says to the other, "I *love* water!" The other fish replies, "What's 'water'?"

What is well known is that those who succeed often build on previous success. Those who have started one business find it easier to start another. We often observe that people whose families are successful are often successful themselves. We can process this phenomenon by inferring that somehow success is "in their blood." But when we limit "success" to such things as occupational prestige, higher education, income, and so on, too often we discount the impact of strong networks and other forms of access that correlate to increased upward mobility for successive generations. As the saying goes, it's not *what* you know, it's *who* you know! Of course, this expression is overly simplistic—and good connections alone rarely are enough for prolonged success in any field.

The truth is that there is a range of invisible factors that give some an unequal advantage on the entrepreneurial playing field. Successful entrepreneurs, the data show, have a toolkit of skills, knowledge, networks, and experiences that tend to be more abundant in some communities than others, but the all-important mix of these tacit assets is the invisible capital (or lack thereof) that helps or hinders entrepreneurial viability.

Let me be clear: invisible capital is not a proxy for racism, sexism, classism, xenophobia, or heterosexism. People who are on the receiving end of one or more of these "isms" are not powerless, nor are they devoid of invisible capital. Indeed, they have the capacity to build invisible capital strategically despite the clear social liabilities they may bear through no fault of their own.

Invisible capital is also no substitute for the entrepreneurial trinity of hard work, ingenuity, and mental fortitude. But these qualities are often prerequisites rather than predictors of sustained viability in business.

Invisible capital is not simply how big your Rolodex is or how many times you've traveled to Europe. It is not just knowing what EBITDA stands for, knowing how to dress when meeting a loan officer, what degrees you've earned, or the level of your digital literacy. It is *all* of those things.

Anyone can acquire invisible capital. Depending on the entrepreneurial opportunity, which aspects of invisible capital you need and in what proportion may change dramatically. Let's look at some examples.

### Tom and Don

Tom's got the million-dollar idea, the work ethic, and the technical skill to make the next big thing since the Snuggie. Yet somehow the stars have not aligned for him as he had hoped (or expected). He attended one of Robert Kiyosaki's *Rich Dad, Poor Dad* seminars, bought an Inventor's Starter Kit after he saw that commercial featuring the caveman cartoon character chiseling a wheel out of a block of stone, put up a cool website that he made from a template offered by his local Yellow Pages company, and tirelessly toils in his mother's garage—

the entrepreneurial place of origin of all proto-billionaires, if we are to believe such things. But to no avail.

Tom has built a cool prototype, but he is having difficulty raising money to build a fully functional one, which is also keeping him from applying for a patent. Tom has no real nest egg to tap, doesn't own a home, and has maxed out his credit cards.

Tom was born in Albania and came to America as a teenager. He and his mother sought political asylum here, having fled the conflict in Kosovo. They migrated to Waterbury, Connecticut, where he graduated from high school. Tom found a decent job working as a technician at an auto repair chain not far from the apartment complex where he rents a studio.

Tom is an industrious, able-bodied White guy with a degree, a job, and a strong work ethic. So what's the deal?

At twenty-three, though, Tom still has a thick accent, dons a *taqiyah* (a Muslim prayer cap), and has poor writing skills (in English, anyway). He has had little exposure to entrepreneurship other than what he sees on cable TV and the local businesses and chain stores he patronizes near where he lives and works. But Tom believes in the American Dream and knows all too well that as daunting as it has been to acclimate to American life, it is head and shoulders above growing up poor in rural Albania.

Tom has sparse invisible capital, but he doesn't know it. And, of course, he doesn't know what invisible capital is and why he needs to have it.

Tom's interpersonal skills are hampered by his poor language and writing skills, and perhaps by people's discomfort with, if not outright prejudice against, his accent and Muslim garb. He has a limited social network because he moved here from Albania and doesn't know how to mine the network he does have (Albanian immigrants, fellow Muslims).

Like Tom, Don is the child of fairly recent European immigrants. He, too, aspired to be an entrepreneur beginning at a young age. Like Tom, his work ethic was stellar. Over the years, Don has developed a couple of marketable skills, and he may even have had a good idea once in a blue moon. That said, Don is no rocket scientist.

But here's where the similarities end. Don grew up in the United States and acquired excellent language and writing skills. While Tom earned a GED and took some classes at his local community college, Don received an MBA from one of the top business schools in the country: the Wharton School at the University of Pennsylvania.

Tom was able to use his mom's small garage to work on his invention; Don landed a job right out of college at a successful real estate development company in his native New York City. Don was able to use that choice job as a professional springboard to greater entrepreneurial opportunity. How did Don land such a prime gig right out of college? Well, he had his newly minted credentials as an Ivy League graduate with highly marketable skills—but he also had the benefit of knowing the owner of the company: his dad.

Yes, I'm referring to The Donald, Mr. Donald Trump, a man who was born on third base and swore he had hit a triple.[1] A man whose biggest success in business came when he accepted a multimillion-dollar inheritance from his father.

## Horatio Alger Didn't Bootstrap It

The original progenitor of bootstrappism was a second-generation Harvard graduate, Horatio Alger Jr. It's likely that young Horatio never in fact wore boots but was born with Ferragamo baby booties. And if he did wear boots, they were surely accompanied by the literary shovel he so deftly wielded as a novelist who popularized the myth of "rugged individualism." Donald Trump and his partner in entrepreneurial myth-weaving, Robert Kiyosaki of *Rich Dad, Poor Dad* merchandising prowess, are Horatio Alger pimps. The subtext of everything they sell is: you can be like us. Sure, you can be just like them if you can access and leverage the same high-powered social networks they did. Kiyosaki and Trump love to talk about the many things would-be and new entrepreneurs need to know (and often already *do* know prior to buying their books)—except for the most important thing: the role of invisible capital. Since the playing field is not level, would-be entrepreneurs who were not born with Ferragamos on their feet first need to identify and build up their invisible capital if they want to have a chance of success.

Kiyosaki's anti-education, anti-elite framework would be just laughably ironic if it wasn't so fundamentally cynical. Trump's and Kiyosaki's entrepreneurial successes are based on merchandising their public personas by leveraging capital they either accessed or expanded through their families or through dubious marketing alliances—a circumstance that neither of them acknowledges nor emphasizes when teaching others "the art of the deal."[2]

As we will see in chapter 4, the vacuum that is entrepreneurial illiteracy is the context that allows media outlets like PBS and other institutions to air a program featuring the *Rich Dad, Poor Dad* nonsense, either not knowing or not caring that they are validating Kiyosaki's self-serving agenda.

Kiyosaki's words are simple, humorous, and counterintuitive. It is easy to believe they come from a good place. Sadly, they don't. But with the PBS imprimatur, Kiyosaki has become mainstream. His verbal alchemy continues to generate hollow directives whose best bits are repurposed (without attribution) from greater minds and whose most stunningly inane advice comes from his venerable "rich dad," whom none of the various investigative journalists on his trail has yet to prove existed!

Why would PBS do such a thing, given its stellar reputation and lofty values that promote critical thought and public discourse? Besides needing money like any other organization, of course. I suspect that most of the decision-makers at PBS are as entrepreneurially illiterate as the viewers they have punished in this rare instance of profoundly bad judgment.

It's intentionally deceptive for entrepreneurship evangelists to belittle or deny the existence of invisible capital. It's professionally irresponsible for reputable journalistic outlets to validate tripe such as Kiyosaki's without properly contextualizing it. But most tragic of all, it is an entrepreneurial death sentence to consume this drivel with the expectation that, armed with the pluck, luck, and virtue espoused by Horatio Alger and the *Rich Dad, Poor Dad* board game, you're ready to conquer the entrepreneurial world. Simply put, if you don't have or seek to build invisible capital, I don't recommend pursuing entrepreneurship—particularly if you are trying to build a scalable and sustainable enterprise.

The odds are already stacked against *any* nascent entrepreneur, as we've seen in the first two chapters of the book. Even The Donald can attest to this frightful probability as a multiple bankruptcy-filer himself, despite his clear unearned advantages as a man, White, born wealthy, and the advantages he leveraged from these factors, such as an elite education and the training, exposure, and connections that came with it.

The question here is not whether smarts and hard work are irrelevant or unimportant. The issue is rather: whose smarts and hard work are more relevant and valued than others? If all Americans had the same chances The Donald was given from birth, invisible capital would not exist.

The Donald did what any enterprising person would do to get ahead: he took full advantage of his skills, resources, and chutzpah to become the author of his own fate (and several popular books). What is unknowable, however, is whether there would even be a Trump empire had he not been born with the trump card of vast invisible capital. Perhaps. But would his ascent be as likely? Hardly.

My maternal grandfather played the stock market for most of his adult life. He used to say with great pride that it paid for most of his five children's college educations. My grandfather lived a charmed middle-class life despite growing up in Jim Crow Baltimore. He was the youngest of seven children, and was a spoiled mama's boy through and through (by his own admission). He inherited some properties from his mother, who was the business manager of her father's highly successful catering business. However, another uncle encouraged him to diversify his investments and look into the stock market.

Following up on that advice, he went downtown to the headquarters of a major investment house. He had no appointment. When a young associate went to the lobby to see him, he was shocked to see a Black man waiting there and was about to shoo him away for fear of hurting his and his firm's reputation by taking on a Black client. Just as my grandfather was being unceremoniously nudged out of the office, the associate's boss's boss walked by and recognized him.

My grandfather greatly resembled his own father, a high school principal and civic leader in the Black community whom the senior manager was acquainted with. The manager, sensing what the associate was about to do, insisted that he take my grandfather on as a client.

The rest is history.

My grandfather had abundant invisible capital, but it almost wasn't enough in that instance. Had the senior manager not walked by just at that moment, perhaps he never would have gotten into the stock market. Yes, part of this story is the role that dumb luck plays. He succeeded not just by showing up on that day, but by possessing the kind of invisible capital that edged out the grave liability of being Black in a traditionally all-White setting. His successful feat on that day was not born out of hard work, ingenuity, or the triumph of optimism; his good fortune stemmed from the fact that he was born into the right family, even though his race was of little to no advantage to him in this context.

If Woody Allen is right and just showing up is indeed 90 percent of success, then some portion of that must be attributed to the invisible capital that informs us where, when, how, and why to show up in the first place.

Without equality of opportunity, we don't know what (or who) represents "the best" (whether it's real estate moguls, scholars, or bloggers). We can only safely know what the best of the rickety system we have inherited produces—along with those rare but highly visible exceptions society uses to validate the rule.

## What Kind of Capital Is It?

To fully acknowledge the importance of invisible capital in expanding opportunity for entrepreneurs, it's vital to understand more about the different types of capital that constitute invisible capital. Invisible capital is not one thing; it's a set of tacit assets that are invaluable to aspiring entrepreneurs. Invisible capital includes economic capital, cultural capital, social capital, and what is often, in macroeconomic and corporate circles, termed human capital. In the context of entrepreneurship, I use the term "human capital" to encompass a broad set of skills and training that have real value in the workplace and professional advancement. But before I delve further into this grab bag I call invisible capital, let me briefly discuss the word *capital* itself.

At first glance, capital is just a synonym for money. But it's not. Capital is something whose value resides only in its ability to create wealth or other wealth-producing assets. Traditional definitions of capital focus on economic capital. They include monetary investments, real estate, production equipment, and intellectual property. Economic capital is certainly helpful in building a business. In the example of Tom and Don, Tom has very little of this traditional kind of capital. His real estate is limited to his mother's garage; his intellectual capital is limited to his unpatentable idea;[3] and he has no financial investments to speak of. Don, on the other hand, was able to leverage his considerable inheritance from his father's extensive real estate holdings, plus whatever assets he had independent of this windfall.[4]

Clearly, old-fashioned capital is immensely useful to all entrepreneurs. But there are other types of capital. We should consider as capital the assets we bring with us from birth and childhood—our race, ethnicity, language of origin, gender, sexuality, religious background, and socioeconomic status. These characteristics are ascribed; they are aspects of ourselves that we cannot change.

To go back to Tom and Don, Don brought with him the kind of capital that is highly valued in our society: he was a White, English-speaking heterosexual Christian male, and came from a wealthy background with elite formal education. Tom, on the other hand, was a White, Albanian-speaking Muslim immigrant from a working-class background.

Luckily for would-be entrepreneurs, invisible capital is not limited to economic capital, or entrepreneurial success would be even less likely than it already is. Entrepreneurs also need what can be called *cultural, human,* and *social* capital. These kinds of capital can be acquired, though some more easily than others. They are types of capital within our control, no matter how you were raised. That said, our ascribed attributes still significantly influence to a greater or lesser degree what kind of cultural capital we build organically, and equally so, the probability of our accessing the cultural capital from our higher-status peers.

Groundbreaking French sociologist Pierre Bourdieu popularized what we call cultural capital. Bourdieu defined cultural capital as our educational qualifications. It is the *embodied* value of what we learn, formally or informally, and is represented by where we went to college and by the degrees we received. Bourdieu developed the idea of cultural capital precisely because he disputed the notion of a society where perfect competition or "perfect equality of opportunity" existed. He wrote, "It is in fact impossible to account for the structure and functioning of the social world unless one reintroduces capital in all its forms and not solely in the one form recognized by economic theory."[5]

For the purposes of this book, I am defining *human capital* as the toolkit of skills and knowledge primarily but not exclusively provided by formal educational or vocational training. Human capital can be acquired through classes, books, informal and formal conversations, directed or independent research, and the most old-fashioned form of human capital acquisition: doing (aka experience). Of course, the specific kind of human capital you're interested in obtaining may necessitate the kind of cultural capital you simply do not have and may not even know exists.

This quandary is bound up with what is perhaps the most complex form of capital of all to understand: *social capital*. And it is arguably the most significant.

It's not *what* you know, it's *who* you know, as the cliché goes. In entrepreneurship, as in other fields (except perhaps politics), we find that it's both, with human capital being a proxy for what one knows and social capital for who one knows. Cultural capital sums up the experience afforded by access to the people you need to know, and economic capital is simply the money it takes to build the three forms of capital mentioned above, or to recruit others who possess at least one of them to help you.

Social capital can best be understood as the set of networks each of us has. Networks are formal or informal groups of people who share one or more affiliations, whether scholastic, religious, vocational, ethnic, geographic, athletic, and so on. Some of these affiliations may be less substantive than others, but that doesn't mean these relationships are not genuine and potentially valuable in business. Robert Putnam, the noted scholar and author of the celebrated book *Bowling Alone*, explains the power of social capital this way:

> No doubt the mechanisms through which civic engagement and social connectedness produce such results—better schools, faster economic development, lower crime, and more effective government—are multiple and complex. While these briefly recounted findings require further confirmation and perhaps qualification, the parallels across hundreds of empirical studies in a dozen disparate disciplines and subfields are striking. Social scientists in several fields have recently suggested a common framework for understanding these phenomena, a framework that rests on the concept of social capital. By analogy with notions of physical capital and human capital—tools and training that enhance individual productivity—social capital refers to features of social organization such as networks, norms, and social trust that facilitate coordination and cooperation for mutual benefit.[6]

Let's use Tom again as an example. Tom might have been able to find his start-up money if he had asked members of his local mosque for help. Or he might have been able to find a lending society of Albanian immigrants who pool their money and give each other microloans for new ventures (an effective way of growing and distributing economic capital used by various immigrant communities).[7] Tom's problem was that he didn't even realize he needed this kind of social capital. The invisible part of human capital is not that entrepreneurs think that starting a business is a skill-free endeavor, but that many underestimate, do not acknowledge or anticipate, or are simply unaware of the several different types of capital necessary to establish sustainable ventures.

Few people emphasize this point better than Michael E. Gerber, author of the underground best-selling entrepreneurs' bible, *The E-Myth Revisited*, who goes to great lengths in his book to dispel the myth that it is simply enough to want it—"it" being to start and run a successful business—without thoughtfully addressing the critical mix of skills and orientations required to effectively manage a business.[8] Gerber's contention is that most would-be entrepreneurs go into business to commercialize a narrowly defined technical or vocational skill they have developed, such as the practice of law, accounting, medicine, cooking, cleaning, designing, or braiding hair. The sad fact, as Gerber is quick to point out, is that some of the most important skills required to excel in business involve human capital that many entrepreneurs don't have and may even refuse to acknowledge are vital, such as marketing, operations, sales, and so on. To quote Gerber:

> Sarah's business was named All About Pies. . . . But in truth, Sarah's business wasn't really all about pies—it was really all about work. The work Sarah did. The work Sarah used to love to do more than anything else. Plus the work Sarah had never done in her life.[9]

Invisible capital is necessary for success. What mix of capital an entrepreneur needs, however, will vary depending on the entrepreneur's venture. That's one of the reasons invisible capital is so, well, *invisible.*

## Inborn Advantages

Cultural capital, generally speaking, is linked to your *ascribed* characteristics—not biologically as some eugenics proponents assert, but as a consequence of the status conferred on you by society at birth. Social capital and human capital are definitely *achieved* characteristics. The Donald, for instance, was born White, male, and rich. None of those attributes was of his making. He did, however, *choose* to apply, attend, and commit to graduate from Wharton. It was this interconnected set of ascribed and achieved assets that greatly boosted Donald Trump's entrepreneurial opportunities.

*Ascribed* characteristics include your race, gender, and class as well as your age, birthplace, nationality, mother tongue, early education, innate temperament, family structure and size, and early exposure to entrepreneurship. These are all characteristics over which you and I have no control. They were decided *for* us—not *by* us.

*Achieved* characteristics flow from the choices we have made, largely from options that were available to us, such as continuing education, occupation, work experience, marital status, financial sophistication, and access to wealth and to potential partners and employees. Some of these factors are more influenced by the circumstances of our birth than others. However, we do have control over our achieved characteristics because they are based largely on decisions we make as we mature.

We are still far from the day when all Americans have the same practical range and quality of choices that the Founding Fathers at least rhetorically evangelized. Sexism, racism, heterosexism, and a batch of other "isms" still exist. Culturally, there remain both male-oriented and female-oriented entrepreneurial pursuits. Construction companies and auto repair shops, for instance, are overwhelmingly male. Beauty salons and day cares, on the other hand, are overwhelmingly female. While much has changed for the better since the sociopolitical upheavals of the 1960s, there still exist real disparities born of legally codified and socially accepted forms of discrimination, as well as continuing bias among people who are the gatekeepers of our economy and society at large.

Clearly, historical and institutional practices continue to influence the modern entrepreneurial sphere. However, if we allow ourselves to scratch the surface, we can see an array of overlapping considerations that deserve greater scrutiny. I don't mean to unduly minimize the powerful role that opportunity plays in entrepreneurial success, but equally important is the issue of capacity, which is not wholly distinct from opportunity. As economist Hernando de Soto points out:

> They forgot what gives an edge to a particular group of people is the innovative use of a … system developed by another culture. For example, Northerners had to copy the legal institutions of ancient Rome to organize themselves and learn the Greek alphabet and the Arabic number symbols and systems to convey information and calculate. And so, today, few are aware of the tremendous edge … given [to] Western societies. As a result, many Westerners have been led to believe that what underpins their successful capitalism is the work ethic they have inherited … in spite of the fact that people all over the world all work hard when they can.[10]

### Does Cancer Cause Smoking?

No, it doesn't. Even silly to ask, isn't it?

Yet in some circles, people believe that whiteness may very well cause success! Or more radically, success causes whiteness. (Insert gratuitous Michael Jackson joke here.) However, race and gender are *not* actually among the top predictors. The more important question is: What is most strongly linked to these factors? This question in itself opens up a host of problems about which innumerable books have already been written.

So, what assets does an aspiring entrepreneur need to survive, let alone thrive, in twenty-first-century America? Of the myriad things to put in that toolbox, I would probably leave out whiteness, maleness, and affluence, despite the varying degrees of usefulness they may have in specific situations. In a country with seemingly intractable disparities that continue to fall along socioeconomic and cultural lines, it is too easy to make race, class, and gender simplistic proxies for the type of invisible capital from which successful entrepreneurs must benefit.

Just as I don't believe that cancer causes smoking, I firmly dispute that entrepreneurial success causes whiteness. We'd do well to remember a basic principle of logical argument, the fallacy of thinking that just because B comes after A, B must have been caused by A. Just because many smokers eventually get cancer doesn't mean that cancer causes smoking. Similarly, just because many White men are successful doesn't mean that all successful entrepreneurs must be White, or that "only White straight men can succeed in America."

White straight guys do have advantages in many, if not most, contexts. For example, women and members of various non-White ethnic groups, with only a few notable exceptions, still have not had great success in breaking the glass ceiling between their midlevel offices and the CEO's executive suite. Yet there are also situations where being a White, heterosexual man can be a distinct disadvantage, and I don't just mean that White, monolingual straight guys should avoid trying to start a Spanish-only speakers bureau for Latinas or a birthing center for lesbian feminist couples.

Madison's story gives a good example of how our preconceptions about what tacit assets will lead to success can be so wrong.

Madison, twenty-three, learned about London's punk rock scene after channel-surfing in her dorm room one Saturday night while a senior at Harvard. She landed on a show that documented punk rock's origin and various influences. Something about it just fascinated her on a primal, even anthropological level.

For the next several weeks, Madison immersed herself in research on the topic. By the end of fall semester, she was a walking punk rock encyclopedia cloaked in meticulously preppy Gossip Girl attire.

Madison had visited London many times on shopping adventures with her mother, but she had never ventured into the shadowy counterculture world that she now knew so well from her intensive reading of all things punk. And then it dawned on her: instead of backpacking across South Africa after graduation, she would open up a London-based punk tourism business.

Madison would graduate Phi Beta Kappa in economics. She had worked in her uncle's venture capital firm for the past two summers as an intern and had experience running several successful large-scale entrepreneurial initiatives for her sorority over the past three years. Madison had the tenacity of a bulldog and was always known for thinking on her feet.

By winter break, Madison had a comprehensive business plan worked up with a full set of financial statements quantifying every aspect of her enterprise-to-be. There was just one hitch: in order to secure a sustainable competitive advantage over her future rivals, Madison knew that she had to somehow get the blessing and strategic involvement of key punk icons and club owners in London.

Madison looked like she had just walked off the set of *Legally Blonde*. She was American, patrician, Ivy League, and the embodiment of all the things that punk rockers despised most. Did this mean that Madison's entrepreneurial endeavor would fail? Not necessarily. But would you bet on her success? I doubt it.

Madison had a LearJet full of invisible capital, but within this set of tacit assets, which things worked for her and which worked against her? And, most important, which would take precedence? In this case, Madison's affluent status, educational credentials, social networks, and nationality did not work to her advantage. What Madison needed most was "street cred," a network of punk icons and club owners—things she did not have.

Being rich, White, male, and Ivy-educated is not enough to achieve (sustained) entrepreneurial success. I'm not saying these characteristics are inherent liabilities; just that, separately or jointly, they're no magic formula for success.

How large or enduring might the disparities be between, say, White women and Puerto Rican men if we leveled these demographic groups' work experience, formal education, income, and household wealth? Let's look at another example.

Dick and Jane graduated together from the same technical school in computer animation. They are both amazing animators. They both want to start their own animation firms, but Jane has an older brother who is an accountant and a mother who is an attorney. Who's more likely to succeed? There are innumerable factors that help or hinder an entrepreneur's range and quality of opportunity.

Dick was born with ... an advantage: he's a man in a man's world, a country where there are twice as many male business owners as women, working in a field that is very much male dominated. These things are nontrivial, but they are by no means predictive of Dick's chances as an entrepreneur. Essentially, these variables are not unlike welcome mats for Dick; they symbolize a fairly wide-open pathway, free of many obstacles that might otherwise have presented themselves solely based on things that Dick could not control, such as his gender, race, sexual orientation, nationality, the family he was born into, or the language he was taught at home.

In the twenty-first-century entrepreneurial landscape, however, Jane is no longer institutionally hobbled by being a woman, despite ever-present patterns of sexism and misogyny that do not appear to be dissolving as quickly as we would like. In this example, Jane has invisible advantages based on class that Dick does not have: she has family members with the kind of expertise that companies specializing in animation need, but that animators rarely have. Her attorney mother can help her daughter with critical legal work (for free) and put her in touch with friends and colleagues in other fields of law that Jane's business requires but that her mother does not practice. Her accountant brother can help her keep track of finances. He, too, can tap his professional networks on his sister's behalf. In this example, the advantage is all Jane's.

I'm not going to argue that ascribed characteristics don't play a role in entrepreneurial success. Ethnicity, gender, and class do matter. We are still far away from the Rev. Martin Luther King Jr.'s dream of judging people by the content of their characters. There are some assets we're simply born with that influence the set of opportunities presented to us. But these assets do not determine our success; they do not guarantee a particular outcome or path for us, personally or professionally. No one asset can guarantee an entrepreneur's success. (Remember The Donald?)

The reality is that race, gender, and class of origin are not inherent predictors of entrepreneurial viability, though we do need to pay attention to such ascribed characteristics because they are often highly relevant indicators for the degree of societal opportunity and institutional access.

It also needs to be emphasized that systemic forms of discrimination still persist that directly impact different groups' advancement and quality of socioeconomic inclusion. The situation is far better than at any other time in our history, but we have a long way to go to achieve equality of opportunity.

An entrepreneur may not be held back because he is Black and poor, but he will be held back if the result of his being Black and poor is that he went to a low-performing inner-city high school, he has very little access to financial investments or real estate, and his social networks are devoid of people who have either money or societal influence. A person in that position *is* facing an uneven playing field, and has to recognize that he needs to radically increase his human, cultural, and social capital if he's going to succeed.

My father's father's father's father established Rabb's Meat Market in Columbus, Mississippi, some time after the Civil War. Like most family-owned businesses, it lasted just two generations. During the roughly seventy-five years the meat market was in business it grew significantly and allowed my family to prosper despite my great-great-grandfather's illiteracy and the limited formal education acquired by his son and successor, my great-grandfather. What was so amazing about this achievement was that the founder was born into slavery and bought his freedom and that of his family and became the biggest vendor in town amid the most racially hostile environments (and eras) in the United States.

When the business finally folded during the Great Depression, three of my ancestor's six sons who chose to go to college could afford to do so, but were not allowed to go past the tenth grade in their native Mississippi due to the state law forbidding public education for African Americans past that scholastic threshold.

The wealth leveraged for their uplift ended with their matriculation to college. None received an inheritance or benefited from the networks once exploited by their father or grandfather. For Black men in the Deep South at the turn of the twentieth century, they had an abundance of invisible capital that they used for their further advancement and for the benefit of their communities and future generations.

The invisible capital they were born with facilitated the accumulation of invisible capital they would later build. And this cycle has repeated itself over five generations. It would be easy (if not wholly self-congratulatory) to claim that I came from a uniquely gifted family, but our good fortune and progress has as much to do with how each successive generation built on and shared the gift of invisible capital for something beyond ourselves.

## Playing Pygmalion

Most human and cultural capital can be acquired. What many entrepreneurs don't realize is how deeply they must immerse themselves in human and cultural capital to improve their opportunities to excel. Playwright George Bernard Shaw understood both the possibility and the difficulty of using human and cultural capital to level the playing field. It's the subject of his play *Pygmalion* (later made into a terrific musical titled *My Fair Lady*). The play revolves around a bet made between two well-to-do friends, Professor Henry Higgins and Colonel Pickering, as to whether or not a poor English flower girl named Eliza Doolittle could be successfully passed off as a refined society lady by learning upper-class diction and etiquette.

This play is about the power and resonance of cultural capital in society—any society. Eliza Doolittle did not grow up rich or formally educated, nor was she educated informally by her family and other close relations in the ways of the English elite. She did not have the vocabulary, accent, graces, skills, or experiences of her wealthy counterparts, having grown up poor and without formal education, without the opportunity into which her privileged patrician counterparts were born. In other words, Eliza Doolittle had little to no cultural capital (or cultural capital of value in that elite world, anyway).

The wager Higgins and Pickering make is whether, if she were given the right cultural capital, Eliza could become a true peer of society ladies who *embodied* such capital, having been part of this rarefied culture since birth. In Shaw's play the short answer is yes, albeit situationally. However, in the real world, beyond an individual's fine clothes, speech, and table manners, there are innumerable forms of cultural capital that are barely detectable to the untrained eye. It's much harder to "pass" as a well-educated, highly cultured person than you might imagine.

### The Invisible Hand Up

Even in twenty-first-century America, it is highly improbable for a member of the average family in the bottom fifth on the economic ladder to ever make it to the top fifth (or for that matter, the second fifth).[11] Sure, we see plenty of rags-to-riches stories on TV, in the movies, and in print. But these are the sexy exceptions to the far more ugly rule. Economic upward mobility in this country is easier than founding a sustainable business, but it's so much harder than we tell ourselves, and our children, when we blindly accept the American Dream as holy gospel rather than an understandably attractive, albeit highly subjective life goal.

Jeff Gates calls this thinking "Marie Antoinette Capitalism" because its rationale is akin to that infamous queen's historic public admonition, "Let them eat cake."[12] And if this is true of modern American capitalism and the futility of the average American's plans to build substantial wealth, the same can be said of the disconnected capitalists who shout, "Just start a business!" Whether this is Kiyosaki Entrepreneurship or Nike Entrepreneurship, I'm not sure. Either way, they are equally reckless.

Entrepreneurship is not a bumper sticker; it's an economic and cultural phenomenon that deserves the attention and analysis its complexity and impacts demand. This is no less true for invisible capital.

Invisible capital is not transferable. Yet its value is only realized when it is exchanged for something else. It has no intrinsic worth, but instead is what Adam Smith, the iconic founder of what we today know as capitalism, called "that part of a man's stock which he expects to yield him a revenue."[13] In the case of invisible capital, of course, that revenue could include access to knowledge, networks, or other resources that could be exploited to help acquire wealth.

The famous nineteenth-century political economist Henry George defined capital as "wealth devoted to a certain purpose."[14] In his famous treatise on economic opportunity and political democracy, *Progress and Poverty*, he took great pains to draw distinctions between what are mere consumer possessions and what is capital. George explains, for example, that a coat for sale is capital, but not the coat a tailor made for himself to wear. Food in a restaurant is capital, but food in one's pantry is not. But unlike invisible capital, these are material forms of capital—not socially constructed ones attached to an individual's achieved or ascribed characteristics, be they gender or occupational status, education or native tongue. Further distinguishing these forms of capital is the fact that the value of invisible capital is most often determined by people and factors outside ourselves.

Whereas George shows how the tailor decides whether or not his clothing is capital, invisible capital's value is based on the socioeconomic hierarchy of the sector of society in which it has evolved.

Whereas once land ownership and Christian denomination were vital factors in determining the degree of opportunity (to say the least) early Americans were afforded, today's algorithms for meaningful opportunity have shifted as society has become more pluralistic and secular.

Henry George took a contrary approach to that of Adam Smith in valuing capital. George thought that capital follows labor, whereas Smith thought that capital came first. George believed, as do I, that there can be no capital without labor, and without land, no labor. Thus, the natural order of the three factors of production is land, labor, and capital. As George argues, "land" in this context is not meant to be narrowly defined as the dirt under our feet; rather, it represents "all natural materials, forces and opportunities. It is the whole material universe outside of humans themselves."

The point of accumulating capital is most often to produce wealth as Edward Wolff defined it. Invisible capital's real value, however, does not directly affect monetary wealth. No one's prodigious Rolodex or ability to acclimate themselves to high society has a direct impact on their bank account. So, invisible capital, while valuable, is not wealth in and of itself. Its economic value, as George applies the concept of "relative wealth," is based on its potential to "obtain [material] wealth in transactions between individuals (or groups)."

This brief digression into Economics 101 is necessary if only to highlight that invisible capital's worth indeed resides exclusively in its exchange value. Once it's no longer useful in exchange, it loses all value. That depreciation of value as it relates to invisible capital is determined by the vicissitudes of society at large and not by the whim of any individual. And even though it is exchangeable, it is not transferable.

In the case of Eliza Doolittle, her tutor could not simply *transfer* his cultural capital from his brain to hers like some kind of Vulcan mind-meld. She had to *acquire* it, albeit under Professor Higgins's tutelage. Eliza could learn what was proper and what her new patrician colleagues thought was important to know. But her knowledge (and capital) was incomplete because she did not have that *embodied* knowledge that only comes from firsthand experience. Eliza Doolittle was like a spy who undertakes cultural espionage. But her lack of authenticity betrayed her intensive training. She was inauthentic because she was performing a role to which she could not relate experientially. Successful spies in the real world are people who actually come from the places they have infiltrated. And they have successfully insinuated themselves because they are products of the environments in which they have been re-embedded. The fictional character of Eliza Doolittle was successful for the narrow purpose of winning a bet, but her chances of preserving, growing, and leveraging her newfound cultural capital over time in the real world would be slim once her peers discovered her true identity.

The hidden advantages of such things as social access dissipate as the cause of social equity gains strength. As women and people of color began to enter the workforce and institutions of higher education in the 1960s and 1970s, the unearned privilege of whiteness and maleness diminished incrementally—at least in those two sectors.

If invisible capital represents forces that advantage those who possess it over those who do not, then acquiring it is indeed a zero-sum game. Because if those people who didn't have it learned how to recognize it and acquire it (albeit proportionally), *everyone* would have it, and therefore *no one* would have it. In other words, there would be no stealth advantages afforded to one person or group over another. And in this idyllic scenario there would finally exist the perfect equality of opportunity and real meritocracy that only the deeply delusional or profoundly ignorant believe exists today.

Capital is pretty much power materialized. And capital, as Bourdieu described it, can present itself in a variety of forms.

Economic (or financial) capital we understand; it is money or material assets that are directly convertible into money. Human capital, which can be indirectly converted into economic capital in some instances, manifests itself in various forms of educational qualifications. Social capital, which is also convertible based on the social situation, consists of what Pierre Bourdieu calls "social obligations," which in common vernacular are basically connections or who you know—or perhaps who knows you (and how well and what they think of you).

Cultural capital, Bourdieu contends, is unlike either economic or social capital, because both can be possessed and embodied. If the value of what we learn formally or informally can be represented by where we went to college or what degree we received, by *embodying* cultural capital we are essentially internalizing the "external wealth" of such distinctions as evidenced by how we put this capital on display (consciously or not). In other words, cultural capital can be acquired through research and traditional learning. However, *embodied* cultural capital is born of immersion in a social milieu and deeply rooted experience.

It's also worth pointing out that, like Madison in our earlier example, not everyone will benefit from the cultural capital prized by Henry Higgins. Attending a school like Yale or Harvard gives you the cultural capital you need to go into politics or high finance, but you had better attend the Culinary Institute of America if you want your first job in a restaurant to be on the line rather than washing dishes.

To succeed, you first have to know what kind of cultural capital you need for your particular enterprise and industry. However, unless you already have that capital, it will be invisible to you. That is, only the people who have it know they need it. So how can you find out what you need to succeed if you were not born with the proverbial silver spoon in your mouth? One way is to develop and then tap your social networks.

### Homophily, Propinquity, and Other Four-Letter Words

Who you know and have access to in life has a direct and powerful influence on creating and expanding entrepreneurial opportunity. Where you were born, where you went to school, and where you work or go to church, for instance, all help determine with whom you interact and how easily you can access others you don't yet know, but could meet through your various social networks (including Facebook).

Depending on how the term is used, different people think different things about "social networking." To some, the expression (or the image that may come with it) leaves a bad taste in their mouths because it conjures up a picture of a "social climber," someone who pretends to be friendly and interested in others solely to advance themselves socially or professionally. To others, "social networking" automatically relates to the Internet.

Facebook is probably the best example of a social networking website, allowing its over 500 million users worldwide to connect (or more commonly, reconnect) with people online with whom they share certain things in common, like a past relationship, occupation, alma mater, or, as is often the case, "mutual friends." Given how popular Facebook is, "friend" has become a term of art, because there are fewer degrees of separation between strangers. In fact, strangers are "friending" each other every day, linked by one or more other "friends" who are not really friends of Facebook users, but virtual acquaintances who often have not actually met in person.

But as in life, there are "friends" and there are *friends*. While the word may be used haphazardly, it is certain that not all friends are created equal—nor, for that matter, are all professional relationships. Moreover, nascent entrepreneurs who don't even know what relationships they need to cultivate are already at a distinct disadvantage when starting or growing their businesses.

If you haven't heard the term *homophily* before, it is entirely possible you might assume it is a word you would not use in polite conversation. The irony is that homophily often influences with whom you converse and what is considered polite or appropriate. Homophily simply means a preference for seeking out and bonding with folks who are similar to you. It begins to get complex when we probe beneath the surface to determine all the many ways we can define similarity, whether ascribed, like gender, or achieved, like occupation.

*Propinquity* sounds like a genetic disorder. In fact, propinquity is a term common in the field of social psychology and is defined as the physical or psychological proximity—or closeness—between people. But like *similarity*, *closeness* can be ambiguous. The propinquity effect for Jane in the previous vignette is multilayered and should not be downplayed. Jane was born into a family that prized entrepreneurial zeal. Her mother and older brother are self-employed professionals in fields with heavy influence on entrepreneurship. As a consequence of being related to these people, Jane also has a closeness to them—kinship in the biological sense of the word—in addition to the kinship they share vocationally.

Not surprisingly, homophily and propinquity are highly interrelated. One suggests that birds of a feather flock together; the other suggests that where and how they nest, feed, and fly will influence what flocks are formed.

So what does flock formation have to do with entrepreneurial opportunity? As the next chapter will illustrate, the kinds of stakeholders an entrepreneur can bring in as co-founders, partners, investors, or early employees correlates highly to the ascribed attributes of the entrepreneur. More bluntly, entrepreneurs tend to team up with people who look like themselves, notwithstanding that what many entrepreneurs have in common with their founding teams is family, through blood or marriage.[15] This is homophily at work. Moreover, entrepreneurs with high status as defined by ascribed characteristics such as race, gender, and socioeconomic class tend to more easily attract other high-status team members—even when others with seemingly more beneficial achieved traits such as key complementary skills and professional experience would add significant value to the founding team.

The ascribed characteristics of low-status individuals—language, nativity, ethnicity, gender, or sexual orientation, for example—may be considered undesirable and therefore mark some would-be entrepreneurs as "low status" to others with the complementary skills and resources. These prospective entrepreneurs need to find ways to access and collaborate with individuals who have valuable strengths (that is, *achieved* characteristics) where they themselves possess clear weaknesses—strengths that too often for all nascent entrepreneurs are given short shrift when building entrepreneurial teams. Sociologists Martin Ruef, Howard Aldrich, and Nancy Carter published a study with some findings relevant to this point:

> [W]e find that team composition is driven by similarity, not differences. Founders ... appear more concerned with trust and familiarity ... than with functional competence.
>
> ... During team composition, entrepreneurs seek out trusted alters, as well as those with whom they already have strong interpersonal relationships, while avoiding strangers who could bring fresh perspectives and ideas to the organizational founding process.
>
> ... Thus, entrepreneurs' tendency to avoid the inclusion of strangers on founding teams tends to decrease functional diversity and may, in the long run, inhibit the success of new formal organizations.
>
> ... The composition of entrepreneurial founding teams reflects the tendency toward gender, ethnic, and occupational homophily in the contemporary United States.[16]

But this is no small feat. The twin forces of homophily and propinquity make it exceptionally challenging for individuals to engage with people who do not look or act like them, or live or otherwise interact with them—especially if they don't have acquaintances who themselves are connected to potential business partners, key employees, vendors, or investors. In the 1996 movie *The Associate*, for example, Whoopi Goldberg and Dianne Wiest go to great lengths to pretend their start-up investment firm in Manhattan is owned and operated by a fictitious high-status financier named Robert S. Cutty in order to improve their chances of successfully operating in the rough-and-tumble, male-dominated, and predominantly White Wall Street investment banking arena.

Thanks to invisible capital, there is a strong correlation between high-status people and the key benefits that founding entrepreneurial teams need to improve their business viability. We would like to think that in the twenty-first century we no longer need to secure someone from a high-status group—particularly when the founding team believes it has the essential competencies to operate a business well. But competencies are one thing, and invisible capital quite another.

Remember, Whoopi Goldberg's character was not a janitor in *The Associate*; she was a highly skilled investment banker who was the genius behind its successful operation. The mythical, never-seen Cutty character (whom she ultimately had to inhabit—literally) was the external validator of her skills and experiences. Cutty was the physical embodiment of invisible capital—something that her entrepreneurial firm desperately needed when her hard work, competency, and perseverance were not enough.

Of course, *The Associate* was just a movie—and a comedy at that. But its lesson is all too real. It was based on a cultural phenomenon that still exists for entrepreneurs (and employees as well) who through no fault of their own are situationally or universally devalued as low status.

Nearly a century ago, my great-grandfather was a self-employed teamster. More specifically, he was a hauler of lumber in Louisville, Kentucky. He had first started in business with a team of horses before the advent of the automobile. Years later he acquired a flatbed truck, which replaced the horses. His father was a veteran of the Civil War, having served in the Union Army as a sergeant in the U.S. Colored Troops before being mustered out when his tour of duty was over. My ancestor was a very light-skinned Black man whose face in the photographs I grew up looking at always resembled Abraham Lincoln to me.

As the story goes, he had finished hauling lumber to one of his repeat customers (all of whom were White) on a hot summer day, and he removed his hat to wipe the perspiration from his forehead. His client was aghast to see the tight curls of his hair, clearly confirming that my great-grandfather was indeed a Black man. Immediately realizing what had transpired, he quickly put his hat back on and left the scene immediately. As my grandmother used to tell the story, her father never took his hat off around clients thereafter, and the customer who took offense at his unintentional disclosure never brought up the affront to his delicate racial sensibilities.

This was, no doubt, an early-twentieth-century version of "Don't ask, don't tell." My great-grandfather was somehow able to put the toothpaste back into the tube, perhaps because his services had greater value than the amount of invisible capital he lost that fateful day. Another way of looking at this same true story is that my great-grandfather gained invaluable cultural capital from it. He acquired a form of knowledge from the harrowing experience of almost losing an important client for flagrantly (though unintentionally) revealing the fact that he was African American in a commercial realm, his Southern Depression-era community, where Blacks were not normally permitted to participate.

Those entrepreneurs with low status who do not have access to high-status individuals because they are not within their preexisting social, civic, or professional networks disproportionately tend to go it alone. The consequences of low-status entrepreneurs pursuing solo endeavors are manifold, and almost universally negative, creating a self-fulfilling prophecy of diminished business viability in terms of organizational growth, longevity, and profitability.[17] Simply put, these nascent entrepreneurs haven't had the social or professional networks to work with, or haven't otherwise been able to meet potential high-status team members or key employees with the invisible capital that can help the venture endure and thrive.

This means that low-status entrepreneurs—individuals who have little formal education, have been incarcerated, are disabled, speak English as a second language, live in rural or inner-city areas, or have other ascribed traits that society generally looks down on—have far fewer meaningful opportunities to improve their firms' business viability compared to their high-status counterparts.

## The Power of Social Networking

We have an image of the relentless American entrepreneur as a man who starts out with a great idea and emerges from his garage with a revolutionary new widget around which a whole industry will rise. But in reality, the rugged solo entrepreneur does not enjoy well-documented advantages that his team-based counterparts benefit from, including the firm's ability to innovate and the value derived from increased social and psychological support in an economic climate that is nothing less than brutal. Here's a story that defies common sense—until we understand the invisible capital that makes it work.

Some of the most ubiquitous businesses in Black urban neighborhoods are Korean-owned beauty supply stores that cater specifically to Black consumers. Unenlightened politicos and media pundits often chalk up this dynamic to the immigrant work ethic and immigrants' inherent entrepreneurial zeal. Or, more to the point, that immigrants work while (domestic) Black people complain. The facts tell a very different and nuanced story.

On the surface, it seems ironic that Korean Americans would have a lock on products that are made for African Americans. But if you look at the labels of many of the products in their stores, you will see that they are made in Korea. Additionally, it is worth specifying that it is not *Asian* Americans who are disproportionately entrepreneurial or self-employed, it's *Korean* Americans in particular. While not knowing—or seeing the value in—this important distinction may reveal a lack of understanding about the entrepreneurial landscape or insight into ethnic clusters in certain professional arenas, this ignorance keeps the Korean American community's unique invisible capital hidden in plain sight.

Much research has been done on the urban entrepreneurial endeavors of Korean immigrants to the U.S. over the decades. Yet little of that research has reached the general public and the corporate media that unduly influence it. Essentially, the overrepresentation of Korean immigrants in largely Black urban local economies boils down to supply, demand, and the invisible capital that links them. Korean American business owners enter markets where they do not have to create demand, just meet it. On the supply side, they are uniquely better positioned to provide products that are made in (or imported from) Korea than Anglo-Americans, Latinos, African Americans, or even non-Korean Asian Americans. After all, who is more likely to speak fluent Korean, have commercial ties to Korean companies, and be able to acquire sufficient debt financing or equity investment with no credit history, or to gain access to high-status peers in established local or regional Korean American networks?[18]

In addition to access to start-up capital, Korean immigrants often come with significant formal education, relevant work experiences, and highly transferable skills. They also have a built-in labor force since they often employ family members (whose compensation may not be reported to the IRS or represent a competitive wage). These are all sustainable competitive advantages that are the outgrowths of having invisible capital in this situation. But gaining this edge in the entrepreneurial sphere comes at the cost of being perceived as a low-status job applicant for positions where strong written and verbal skills in English are required—where one needs the cultural capital associated with understanding how to operate in a uniquely American corporate or professional work environment.

Among immigrants who lack a command of standard English and experience living in a socially integrated fashion in the United States, entrepreneurship of this kind is not about the adrenaline rush of risk-taking so often associated with the caricature of the entrepreneur—or even about a deep-seated desire to amass a large fortune. The reality is that entrepreneurship for many immigrants is the most viable vocational option based on the opportunities they have, or believe they can reasonably create for themselves. I also hasten to add that the types of storefront establishments Korean immigrants start are neither high-revenue or high-scale enterprises, and do not create the level of wealth or produce the quality of life one might assume.[19]

The best way to determine whether this is a satisfactory entrepreneurial path would be to find out how many children of Korean immigrant business owners stay in the family business or go on to pursue entrepreneurial ventures. Such research would certainly be very revealing. However, a fair assumption we can already make is that a strong work ethic is almost a defining characteristic of most newly immigrated residents of *all* nationalities—women, men, and children who have often traveled great distances and through harrowing circumstances to find the opportunity our nation purports to provide in abundance. But if hard work alone were the panacea for economic uplift, our country would look and function much differently.

Hard work by itself does not account for the vast disparities that exist between immigrants from the educated merchant class of their homelands and the working poor of America's most economically blighted neighborhoods. Even if institutional racism, urban decay, and rampant violence somehow dissolved overnight, any non-Korean entrepreneurs seeking to compete for that market would fare poorly without the strong cultural and industry ties business-minded Korean immigrants have to the producers and distributors of the beauty products they sell—most notably the wigs and hair extensions so popular with women from Harlem to Hollywood.[20]

If any of this sounds familiar, then you're beginning to get the point: these different forms of capital have a powerful cumulative effect on entrepreneurial opportunity, which in turn impacts entrepreneurial outcomes. These forces are not guarantees of success, but they are the winds that lift your chances of achieving it, should you dare to cast your metaphorical kite to the skies.

Luck and pluck may be invaluable assets for would-be entrepreneurs—particularly when pluck is followed by luck. But pluck alone is not enough. And waiting to get lucky is something I would not suggest mentioning in the executive summary of your business plan.

Invisible capital, however unequally distributed, is neither scarce nor improbable to acquire. But if you don't know what it is, don't know how to get it, don't believe it actually exists, or, worst of all, don't think that invisible capital matters, I have a stringless kite to sell you.

# 4

# Democratizing Entrepreneurial Opportunity

To understand your country you must love it. To love it you must, in a sense, accept it. To accept it as it is, however, is to betray it. To accept your country without betraying it, you must love it for that in it which shows what it might become. America—this monument to the genius of ordinary men and women, this place where hope becomes capacity, this long, halting turn of the no into that yes—needs citizens who love it enough to re-imagine and remake it.

Roberto Mangabeira Unger and Cornel West,
*The Future of American Progressivism*

Democratizing entrepreneurial opportunity simply means fostering real, highly navigable inroads to entrepreneurship from all corners of our society for common benefit. Full and proportional participation in the entrepreneurial sector is within our means to accomplish and is worth achieving for our collective economic and social benefit. Just as disparities in high school graduation and literacy rates between groups have decreased dramatically over the years, it is well within our means and our tradition to provide meaningful access to training and resources for successive generations of American entrepreneurs.

Figure 10 shows that in less than thirty years the gap between the rates of voter registration for Blacks and Whites has all but dis-

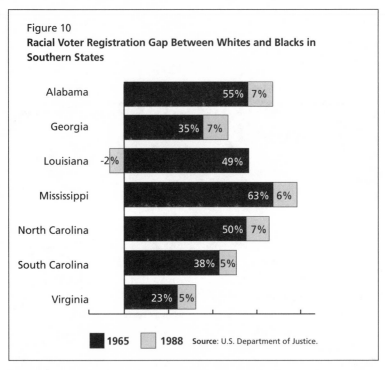

Figure 10
**Racial Voter Registration Gap Between Whites and Blacks in Southern States**

| | 1965 | 1988 |
|---|---|---|
| Alabama | 55% | 7% |
| Georgia | 35% | 7% |
| Louisiana | -2% | 49% |
| Mississippi | 63% | 6% |
| North Carolina | 50% | 7% |
| South Carolina | 38% | 5% |
| Virginia | 23% | 5% |

■ 1965   ☐ 1988   Source: U.S. Department of Justice.

solved in the seven Southern states where from 1865 to 1965 the Black vote was most systematically suppressed, if not outright denied. This seemingly miraculous feat was not due to our federal government leading the way. It was a critical mass of our elected officials and the media who listened to the voices and were inspired by (or perhaps scared by) the actions of ordinary citizens—parents, students, members of the clergy, and others—and demanded equal rights for all. It came too slowly, too gradually, and at the expense of too many innocent lives and irreparable harm to the livelihoods of families from South to North, rural to urban, but we are a better nation because of it.

Indeed, an active and truly representative electorate is a cornerstone of democracy. And a well-trained, well-resourced, and inclusive entrepreneurial class is vital to a vibrant and sustainable market economy, because by the very nature of its diversity and equitable composition it provides a self-regulating force of stakeholders who will encourage growth that is not at the expense of sustainability and shared prosperity.

This is no idealist hope for an entrepreneurial utopia; it is a very real expectation for communities to be the authors of their own respective and intertwined destinies. And equally promising, the past is prologue: we've done it before, and in some cases, we've never stopped doing it. So, what exactly is "it"?

It is many things, and everyone has a role. But certainly a vital component of it is what economist Jessica Gordon Nembhard calls "democratic community economics"[1]—enterprises of all kinds that leverage invisible capital to empower whole communities for collective benefit rather than pure profit-seeking for the individual. For time-tested cooperatives, newly minted benefit corporations (B Corps), and low-profit limited liability companies (L3Cs), innovations in entrepreneurial structures are as powerful as the innovations that entrepreneurship itself may spark.[2]

There is, no doubt, room for all kinds of entrepreneurs and business owners, but broad sustainability for local communities will not be created by mammoth corporations or by following traditional business models—no matter how impressively small their eco-footprints or the number of green jobs they claim to create.

Green jobs—unskilled and semi-skilled jobs that pay a living wage or better—are invaluable and vital to the development of a just, inclusive, and verdant economy. But "green jobs" produced by the likes of infamous coal extractor Massey Energy Company can never make up for the catastrophic and systemic harm such a company does to our economy and to society at large. Green jobs that are created merely to make (or save) another shade of green do little to sustain communities over the long haul. And green entrepreneurship that doesn't in one way or another create or bolster community assets is invisible capital that is poorly leveraged. The same can be said of the policies that promote or provide incentives for entrepreneurship.

We have seen how the policies stemming from the Voting Rights Act of 1965 produced dramatically higher rates of voter registration among previously marginalized citizens, a marginalization reflecting our country's original sins of slavery and institutional racism. Despite seemingly insurmountable odds, civic innovation along the lines of voting rights has corrected an egregious and long-standing inequity by providing equal opportunity and access to the ballot box to let our diverse electorate's voice be heard and embolden our democracy in the process.

We know now that entrepreneurial opportunity is neither democratic nor representative of what scholar Gar Alperovitz aptly calls our "pluralistic commonwealth."[3] But it should be. And the power to make it so is entirely within our hands; we have the collective will to make it happen in our lifetime regardless of what is mistaken for progress on Capitol Hill or Wall Street.

So why doesn't the population of entrepreneurs mirror the rest of the country? Why are so many entrepreneurs failing to succeed? What's not working?

Well, for one thing, to paraphrase a chapter title from Jeff Gates's book *The Ownership Solution*, the problem with capitalism is that it doesn't create enough capitalists—at least, in the strict sense of this term—namely, people who have and accumulate capital.[4]

Look around the entrepreneurial landscape, and you will see all kinds of institutions set up to promote "entrepreneurial success." These entities range from units within the Small Business Administration (SBA) such as Small Business Development Centers (SBDCs) and Small Business Investment Companies (SBICs) to local chambers of commerce, the Service Corps of Retired Executives (SCORE), and the National Federation of Independent Business (NFIB). NFIB is perhaps the single largest shaper of "small business" policy (and widely accepted jargon) in the U.S. But if there's so much support, why do so many businesses fail?

The answer, it will come as no surprise, is that these government agencies, trade associations, and lobbying interests, for all their expertise, consciously or otherwise promote an alarming level of entrepreneurial illiteracy. That illiteracy in turn produces a willful ignorance among a whole host of other institutions whose decisions impact entrepreneurs.

Indeed, there is no lack of comprehensive and credible entrepreneurial research coming out of consortia of universities such as the Entrepreneurial Research Consortium in the U.S. and the Global Entrepreneurship Monitor (GEM), which provides annual comparisons across various countries of measures of new-venture creation activities, as well as invaluable work generated by leading institutions like the Kauffman Foundation.

The research coming out of these organizations paints a picture that is much different from what we have been programmed to believe in the U.S. about entrepreneurship and business formation here and abroad. You might even have been duped to think that *entrepreneurship* is an English word invented by Thomas Alva Edison. It isn't.

In fact, international comparisons show that the richer the nation, the lower the rate of self-employment—a phenomenon in the labor market highly correlated with new venture creation. And as Scott Shane points out in his valuable book *The Illusions of Entrepreneurship*, the self-deceptive webs we weave about entrepreneurship make real determinants of business viability seem invalid—or worse, invisible![5] Shane writes:

Myths about entrepreneurship make finding this information difficult for two reasons. First, the myths imply that many things that actually matter for success really don't matter. For instance, the myths about entrepreneurship tell you that how much money you start with, or the industry in which your business operates, or the legal form of your business, or how many employees you have when you start, or what strategy you adopt don't matter for success. But as it turns out, they matter a lot. Believing the myths might keep you from doing the things that you need to do to succeed.

Second, the myths tell you that many things that actually don't matter will make a difference in terms of the success of a start-up. For instance, the myths about entrepreneurship maintain that having persistence, being self-confident, and being a leader will make you a successful entrepreneur. But there's no good evidence that new businesses founded by people with these characteristics perform any better than other start-ups. Believing these myths might focus your attention on the very things that you shouldn't spend your time on.[6]

Do any of these themes sound familiar to you? Stay positive. Think good thoughts. Just do it! Summon that American "can-do" spirit! These aren't research-based strategies for success, they're slogans to sell you something that will help the seller (in the short term, anyway) and will actually hinder you. It doesn't matter if the seller of these mantras is intentionally deceptive or not, because the effect is the same: encouraging people to start businesses they have no business launching in the first place.

These entrepreneurship boosters might as well be enticing an asthmatic child to climb Mt. Everest by saying there's infinite candy on the summit—and withholding the inhaler! Rather than acknowledge the role of invisible capital, they hawk the glories of America's inherent and unique fabulousness. (Ever notice how every year it seems a U.S. baseball team wins the *World* Series?) These boosters elevate large corporations as the entrepreneur's ideal goal, when the odds of becoming the next Bill Gates are only marginally better than those of winning the lottery. And if you look just a little bit deeper, you will find what's at the heart of entrepreneur veneration: the tunnel vision created by only looking at the victors and conveniently ignoring those who have fallen along the way to justify popular theories of entrepreneurial prowess.

Nassim Nicholas Taleb describes the circular "black swan" logic of many such boosters:

A black swan is an outlier, an event that lies beyond the realm of normal expectations. Most people expect all swans to be white because that's what their experience tells them; a black swan is by definition a surprise. Nevertheless, people tend to concoct explanations for them after the fact, which makes them appear more predictable, and less random, than they are. Our minds are designed to retain, for efficient storage, past information that fits into a compressed narrative. This distortion, called the hindsight bias, prevents us from adequately learning from the past.

Black swans can have extreme effects: just a few explain almost everything, from the success of some ideas and religions to events in our personal lives. Moreover, their influence seems to have grown in the 20th century, while ordinary events—the ones we study and discuss and learn about in history or from the news—are becoming increasingly inconsequential.

The mandate [to predict black swans] is also a prime example of the phenomenon known as hindsight distortion. To paraphrase Kierkegaard, history runs forward but is seen backward.[7]

Not entirely unrelated to this argument, Taleb also has words for the best-selling book *The Millionaire Next Door*, to which he applies the black swan critique. He points out that the methodology its authors use to determine how one becomes a millionaire is unsound, because they only look at the traits of the millionaires and not at all the other people who may share the very same set of traits but have not ended up wealthy. Taleb writes:

What these people forgot to do is to go take a look at the less visible cemetery—in other words, bankrupt people, failures, people who went out of business—and look at their traits. They would have discovered that some of the same traits are shared by these people, like hard work and risk-taking. This tells me that the unique trait that the millionaires had in common was mostly luck.[8]

Again, the matter of luck arises. And everyone seems to have their own definition of it that reveals their own worldview. One saying has is that luck is when preparation meets opportunity. Another is that we make our own luck, which also implies preparedness, or at least initiative. But one of my new favorites was coined by baseball pioneer Branch Rickey: "Luck is the residue of design."

Of course, like so many profound, but irksomely vague, axioms, how the interpreter defines "design" can be as expansive as the Rocky Mountains. And in the context of a society where invisible capital exists, I see Rickey's "residue of design" implicitly acknowledging a craggy terrain better suited for a mountain lion than a cheetah. Who's more likely to "luck out" and catch prey in this environment? Defend herself? Find shelter? A cheetah's fast on the broad plains of southern Africa and strong, but it's no match for the mountain lion in the Rockies. Ultimately, success in any environment is based on agility. And agility—like intelligence—is highly situational. So, too, is invisible capital.

Taleb's critique of *The Millionaire Next Door* essentially rests on the point that its authors have chosen to define wealth-building *agility* in ways that are both unscientific and self-fulfilling because they claim to evaluate all animals' performance when in fact they're just looking at the mountain lions. However, an even more fundamental concern is this: What really are the most important measures of entrepreneurial success?

Certainly a firm's revenues, profit margin, payroll, and longevity are critical variables. But what other important metrics are we leaving out of this assessment that have economic, cultural, and social implications? If the American Dream for entrepreneurs in any real way overlaps with our national mantra "Life, liberty, and the pursuit of happiness," then how do we factor in the quality of life of the founders and employees of entrepreneurial ventures? Moreover, what about how such ventures impact other nonowner stakeholders in a range of ways that don't revolve around short-term material gratification?

This is no bleeding-heart-liberal diatribe against market economies. Market economies are not the culprit, and they predate capitalism, just as merchants, vendors, inventors, and farmers by far predate the adoption of the term "entrepreneur." Not convinced? Just compare the ratio of U.S. CEO compensation to the average worker's salary in 1965 and in 2005. The ratio rises from 24:1 to 262:1, according to Lawrence Mishel of the Economic Policy Institute.[9] This perverse widening of income disparity masks the even greater wealth gaps between those with the most invisible capital and those without it. The culprit is American exceptionalism.

### Exceptionalism Misunderstood

Invisible capital has been *institutionalized,* and its creation did not occur in a vacuum. It was created, configured, and morphed stealthily by institutions, both formal and informal, and reinforced by popular memes broadcast from generation to generation of Americans.

*Memes* are cultural ideas, values, or behaviors that enter our minds in our formative years and often stay with us—most often unconsciously—for a lifetime. Memes are not bad in and of themselves. They are expressions, habits, beliefs that fuse to our psyches. They, too, are invisible until the ultraviolet light of critical thought is cast on them.

A key meme guiding American thought is the gospel of *exceptionalism*. We believe that we Americans are better than any other nation or people—that we are smarter, harder-working, and generally more enlightened than anyone else. American exceptionalism is not all bad, though. It can motivate us to "do better than the Joneses" when the Joneses are India or China and the task at hand is better preparing our high school graduates for the careers of the future (and the present). However, the problem with a meme like exceptionalism is that people actually believe it's true. Far too many Americans actually think that we *are* better than everyone else in the world (overlooking the inconvenient fact that most of us have never traveled abroad or can even locate other countries on a map—not to mention most states within our own borders). What's worse is how "better" is often defined in terms of shallow pleasures and material property, we mistake unbridled consumer choice for social justice and democracy. They are neither.

I hate to break it to my fellow Americans, but in almost every category of entrepreneurial endeavor we are outpaced by our counterparts in the industrialized world. We do not have the most educated citizenry. We may be the richest nation (in terms of our gross domestic product), but we cannot boast that we are the world's most entrepreneurial nation.

In fact, according to the Global Entrepreneurial Monitor's 2005 executive report, the U.S. actually ranks as the twenty-fifth-most entrepreneurial country in the world, with less than one-third the proportion of new and early-stage enterprises per capita of number one–ranked Thailand.

Even when you look at self-employment, the major on-ramp to entrepreneurship, it is worth noting that the U.S. is not even in the top twenty countries that the Organization for Economic Cooperation and Development identifies with the highest self-employment rate. Interestingly, there appears to be a strong *inverse* correlation between the gross domestic product of a nation and its self-employment rate. In other words, the richer the country, the less likely you'll work for yourself. Furthermore, Steven Hipple, an economist at the Department of Labor, has documented how the U.S. can be seen as having become dramatically *less* entrepreneurial if one subscribes to the notion that the self-employed are a subset of or precursor to new venture creation.[10]

Hipple shows that in 1948, nearly one in five (18.5 percent) adult workers were self-employed, contrasted to fewer than one in ten workers (7.5 percent) by 2003.[11] An important exception to this trend is the *incorporated* self-employed sphere, which highly overlaps with owners of microenterprises ("micropreneurs") and "entreprofessionals," including free agents, independent contractors, and other knowledge workers who are "between jobs."

This is not to say that Americans lack ingenuity or enterprise. Far from it. It is, however, something quite different to say that Americans are the *most* industrious or, in more common parlance, that real ingenuity or innovation can occur "only in America."

Such is the power of memes, and in this case the idea of American exceptionalism only works to make invisible capital all the more invisible. After all, if America is the land of opportunity, a place so stuffed with innovation and creativity that anyone should be able to succeed, we have no way of understanding what happens when people don't succeed. We are not trained to do what anyone in business would do when profit goes down, which is to track back through sales reports to see where the problem lies.

What's truly deadly to entrepreneurs is how many people actually have a stake in preventing us from shining a light on invisible capital. These organizations, agencies, and individuals promote American exceptionalism because our belief in that myth enhances their interests, even though it leaves potential entrepreneurs blind and our nation far less prosperous and equitable than it can and should be.

### The Entrepreneurial-Industrial Complex

Some entities feed off the inequities that constitute invisible capital. These hucksters, ideologues, and entrepreneurship cheerleaders represent some of the forces behind what I call the Entrepreneurial-Industrial Complex. They push their agenda by using language, marketing, and politics to paint a picture of an entrepreneurial world that does not really exist.

This is no conspiracy theory. Conspiracy requires a level of formal or informal collaboration that I am not assuming occurs between the various parties at work in this complex. They include formal institutions that have well-funded lobbying operations on Capitol Hill, as is the case with the National Federation of Independent Business, and other groups and individuals that are complicit unknowingly, through their inadvertent behavior, rather than out of ideological fervor.

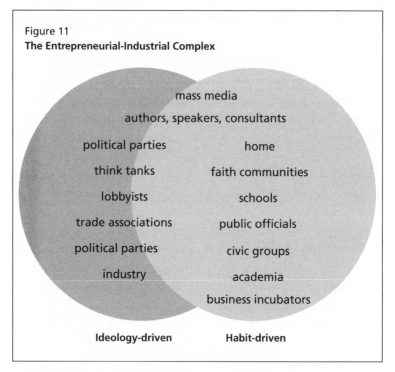

Figure 11
The Entrepreneurial-Industrial Complex

mass media
authors, speakers, consultants
political parties                    home
think tanks                  faith communities
lobbyists                        schools
trade associations              public officials
political parties                 civic groups
industry                       academia
business incubators

**Ideology-driven**              **Habit-driven**

To illustrate the difference between an institutional party and an individual, let's take the example of an urban legend. Pick one—almost any one will do. I got duped by one in 1994 when I was a young U.S. Senate staffer and very new to the Internet. An email was passed along to me that seemed quite credible and highly relevant—so much so I felt compelled to share it at a staff meeting, not realizing that it was in fact a hoax. This was the urban legend that claimed that if you flashed your headlights to warn the driver of an oncoming car whose lights were not on, you could set in motion a gang initiation where the driver of the other car would have to murder you, the good Samaritan, to become the gang's newest member.

I didn't spread that hoax out of malice, but choosing to share this urban legend without verifying it first made me culpable. Of course, the laziness or gullibility associated with my decision to spread this faux news did not make me as responsible as the actual creator of this malicious story, but the damage was done and it was "going viral" with my help.

The same process can be seen in the effects of the Entrepreneurial-Industrial Complex. Every time we accept a myth or outright un-truth as fact, we embolden and become an involuntary part of this complex, whose motives revolve around greed, deception, and fur-therance of beliefs that have little basis in fact and more to do with self-aggrandizement.

When a politician says, "Small businesses are the backbone of our economy," it's as deep as saying, "I believe that children are the fu-ture." It's the cheapest form of pandering because virtually no one will disagree with either statement. If the speaker doesn't first say how he defines the terms he uses, he either intentionally or unknow-ingly allows his audience to interpret his words however it likes. And these slippery generalities often create confusion that mires the issues in such hollow rhetoric that they are much more difficult to address intelligently.

I started working for the White House Conference on Small Busi-ness the very same week in 1994 that the Republican Party won a majority of seats in the House of Representatives for the first time in forty years. The agenda of the nonpartisan commission for which I worked was all but sabotaged shortly thereafter as the Contract *on* America became the guiding document for the new Republican House majority led by Speaker Newt Gingrich.

The commission staff designed a democratic, inclusive, and trans-parent process to ensure that a diverse range of business owners would participate in our state and regional conferences. This pro-cess was shunted aside by the lobbying juggernaut that was (and is) the National Federation of Independent Business. That organiza-tion gamed the system—albeit by legal means—by sponsoring slates composed entirely of candidates affiliated with their group and com-mitted to supporting a program of Republican legislative measures that had been gathering dust since the end of President George H.W. Bush's tenure in the White House.

NFIB had the organized money and the institutional power to override and drown out the various other constituencies in the business community who didn't have strong (or any) lobbying muscle in Washington. It was their agenda that dominated our final report to President Bill Clinton in September 1995, despite our staff's best efforts to represent the broad interests of a far more ideologically and demographically diverse group of entrepreneurs and business owners. And even though much of the legislative agenda they fought for went nowhere during the Clinton era, the language they created around their agenda has been quietly and seamlessly adopted by both parties, the mainstream media, and the public at large ever since.

The power of language in all spheres is significant. In the field of business and entrepreneurship, however, it can be far more sinister because it's cloaked in the rhetoric of our founding documents and our vague but enduring belief in the American Dream, which means something different to everyone except for the idea that it has become our unalienable right to embrace it—whatever "it" may be, including complex, rarely defined ideas such as capitalism, democracy, and free enterprise. The vocabulary? Memes we use every day, such as "small business owners," "free markets," "rugged individualism," "meritocracy," "pulling yourself up by your bootstraps," "self-made," "rags-to-riches," "tax relief," and, my personal favorite, the "death tax."

The NFIB is a "nonpartisan" business association that is the single largest lobbying entity for "small businesses." At least, that's how they represent themselves. But we must remember that what we anecdotally describe as small business rarely encompasses the much larger pool of business owners who by SBA standards can employ up to 500 people. So, Angelo's Pizzeria, with its seven employees, is clearly a *small* business. But how about Angie's List, a popular website that compiles consumer reviews for local service-oriented companies nationwide, with its roughly 400 employees? Not so much. This doesn't mean that most companies with a few hundred employees should be considered the same as businesses like General Electric or Boeing that employ thousands of people—just that there is nothing magical

Figure 12
**Whose Lobbying Muscle Is Strongest on Capitol Hill?**

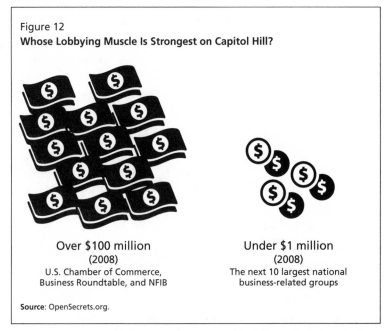

Over $100 million
(2008)
U.S. Chamber of Commerce,
Business Roundtable, and NFIB

Under $1 million
(2008)
The next 10 largest national
business-related groups

**Source:** OpenSecrets.org.

or particularly resonant about the 500-employee mark in the modern American business arena.

Based on the NFIB Issues and Elections page of its website, NFIB appears more aligned with the interests of Reagan-style Republicans than with the average businessperson who employs a handful of employees. NFIB is in fact the highly influential 1943 spin-off of the even more politically entrenched U.S. Chamber of Commerce, which used to boast of having 3 million members until a *Mother Jones* magazine article in 2009 forced it to admit that its membership was much closer to 300,000 (roughly the number of members the NFIB claims).[12]

But regardless of the political ideology the NFIB embraces, it is not safe to assume that its lobbying agenda on Capitol Hill reflects the will or interests of all self-identified small business owners rather than the narrow interests of the self-selected groups of business owners who are drawn to it. Clearly, there are NFIB members who do not necessarily embrace the organization's agenda but become members to take advantage of NFIB's various membership perks or networking. However, I'd also surmise that the Log Cabin Republicans are not politically representative of most LGBTQ community members.[13] If the NFIB does have, say, 350,000 members, that's nothing to sneeze at. But neither are the nearly 28 million Americans who are self-employed or owners of firms with fewer than 500 employees. These people need a voice, too!

The problem with the NFIB and the Entrepreneurial-Industrial Complex is that they promote a "small business" agenda that at best benefits (in the short run, perhaps) that subset of U.S. firms that are technically small by the SBA's definition of the word, but are quite large according to the average person's perception of *small*, as customers of the local, neighborhood-oriented companies people commonly patronize. To the Entrepreneurial-Industrial Complex, "small business" is a term of art meant to mislead people into supporting an agenda—and accepting its accompanying language and assumptions—that we might not otherwise agree to.

But this critique doesn't stop at NFIB's doorstep, among the hordes of K Street lobbyists. In fact, this complex spans the country: from Wall Street and Madison Avenue, through the idyllic Main Streets of Middle America, across the fruited plain to Hollywood and north to Silicon Valley. If the NFIB is the progenitor of much of the policy and language used by entrepreneurially illiterate politicians, then corporate media are the complicit distributors of that package. The handful of major conglomerates that own most of the media we consume via TV, cable, satellite, radio, newsprint, magazines, websites, and movies all to a greater or lesser extent reinforce, both explicitly and subliminally, the myths and hyperbole that entrepreneurship advocates like Scott Shane, Alicia Robb, Rob Fairlie, and Guy Kawasaki so deftly dispel.[14]

This is no conspiracy, just the by-product of a consumption-oriented economy whose most cynical participants have cunningly whipped up a delicious yet toxic cocktail of Horatio Alger fiction, Norman Vincent Peale "positive thinking" quackery, and a healthy portion of Benjamin Franklin–style inventor veneration. It's the holy trinity of propaganda Americana: hard work, a great idea, and a good attitude.

And for the savvy entrepreneurs who excel at duping unsuspecting would-be entrepreneurs into paying them for "the secrets to entrepreneurial success," whether in real estate, appliances, vitamins, hair care, or beauty products, they are rewarded with mainstream validation and exposure. Indeed, you don't even need to have a great idea, just a fancy infomercial or DVD that claims that you do—and maybe you can even get your own PBS special!

## The ABCs of MBEs, WBEs, and SDBEs

Democrats have, over the years, fitfully attempted to address invisible capital through a range of social programs. Recognizing that many women and communities of color have been left out of the entrepreneurial sphere—particularly the government contracting sector, which enriches such companies as General Electric, Lockheed Martin, Halliburton, and Xe (formerly Blackwater)—many Democrats (and the now-extinct liberal Republicans) have tried to create pathways of opportunity by establishing a range of federal programs that reward diversity and inclusion.

Many of these diversity programs began in the wake of the unparalleled social movements of the 1960s. It was the dawn of affirmative action, fair housing, and accommodations laws, the opening up of hitherto virtually all-White and all-male institutions of higher learning, and the broadening of opportunities to do business with the federal government. These causes, laws, and programs were created in a spirit that honored the rhetoric of the Founding Fathers in furtherance of democracy, equality, and broad opportunity. They were, however, created by human beings. So, these efforts weren't—and aren't—perfect.

The categories of Minority Business Enterprises (MBEs) along with Women-Owned Business Enterprises (WBEs) and Small Disadvantaged Business Enterprises (SDBEs) were created to help diversify the pool of federal (and later, state, local, and corporate) contractors

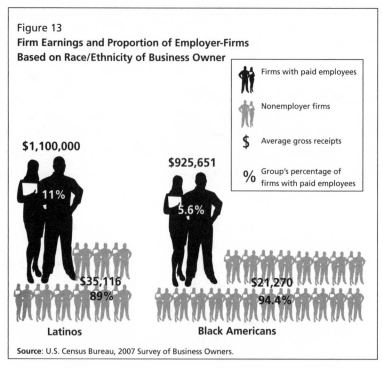

Figure 13
**Firm Earnings and Proportion of Employer-Firms Based on Race/Ethnicity of Business Owner**

Firms with paid employees

Nonemployer firms

$    Average gross receipts

%    Group's percentage of firms with paid employees

$1,100,000

$925,651

11%

5.6%

$35,116
89%

$21,270
94.4%

Latinos

Black Americans

**Source**: U.S. Census Bureau, 2007 Survey of Business Owners.

and vendors. The problem was that these set-aside programs were initially based on good intentions rather than on good data (which at the time didn't exist) to combat rampant patterns of racial and gender discrimination. However, the original sin of these laudable programs was that they fused together two variables that were not always present in or applicable to the beneficiary communities: 1) patterns of racial discrimination against non-White citizens; and 2) underrepresentation of non-Whites within a given industry.

Normally, underrepresentation was a direct consequence of discrimination and exclusion. But with the influx of well-educated immigrant professionals and businesspeople from places like India and China due to a relaxed, "pro-business" immigration policy set into motion by the Immigration and Nationality Act of 1965, it's become apparent that some people of color who face visceral forms of racial discrimination do not necessarily face downward economic or profes-

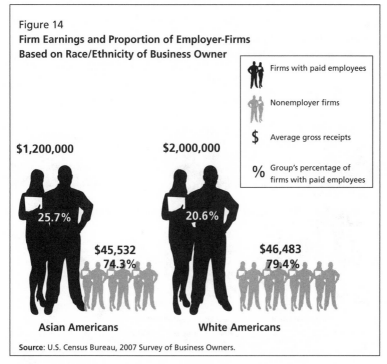

Figure 14
**Firm Earnings and Proportion of Employer-Firms
Based on Race/Ethnicity of Business Owner**

Firms with paid employees

Nonemployer firms

$  Average gross receipts

%  Group's percentage of
firms with paid employees

$1,200,000            $2,000,000

25.7%                 20.6%

$45,532              $46,483
74.3%                79.4%

Asian Americans      White Americans

Source: U.S. Census Bureau, 2007 Survey of Business Owners.

sional mobility, as government data on income, wealth, and business formation since the 1960s clearly indicate.[15]

In other words, some "non-White" people were and are far more disadvantaged than others. And when it came to entrepreneurial opportunity, highly skilled immigrants with significant invisible capital fared better than the average White business owner. There is no better example of this dynamic than Silicon Valley's high-tech industries.

And here's where things start to get tricky. Indian Americans (not to be confused with American Indians) and Japanese, Chinese, and Korean Americans, for instance, have higher rates of self-employment and business formation than the national average and White Americans. They are more likely than their non-White counterparts to have businesses that are incorporated, that have payrolls, and that employ more than 500 paid workers.[16] Asian Americans are clearly a

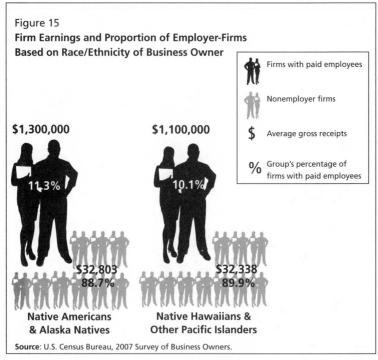

Figure 15
Firm Earnings and Proportion of Employer-Firms
Based on Race/Ethnicity of Business Owner

Firms with paid employees

Nonemployer firms

$ Average gross receipts

% Group's percentage of firms with paid employees

$1,300,000

11.3%

$32,803
88.7%

Native Americans
& Alaska Natives

$1,100,000

10.1%

$32,338
89.9%

Native Hawaiians &
Other Pacific Islanders

Source: U.S. Census Bureau, 2007 Survey of Business Owners.

numerical minority of the U.S. population, at 4.4 percent in 2008, but in the context of entrepreneurial opportunity and business formation, including them among MBEs is both confusing and unfruitful, despite the fact that Vietnamese, Laotian, and Hmong Americans, for instance, have more in common with Black and Latino business owners than they do with other, much higher performing Asian American firms, such as Indian-American and Korean-American enterprises. The same can be said when comparing two Latino populations: Puerto Ricans and the overwhelmingly more affluent Cuban Americans.

Rates of business formation, size, and viability, however, do not in themselves prove or disprove the influence of other less savory forces on female business owners or entrepreneurs of color. Racial and gender discrimination persists over half a century after some of the most sweeping social changes occurred in our nation, fomented by such emblematic protests as the 1955 Montgomery Bus Boycott in Alabama (organized largely by women).

But formal recognition of past or current structural inequalities based on race, nationality, and gender is not the same thing as inclusiveness. When we make these two different, but interrelated, matters synonymous, bad things happen. And when we let them marinate for a few decades, we get problems that are much harder to correct. As I showed in chapter 3, race too often serves as the convenient proxy we use as a nation to represent a vast array of different variables, a discrete subset of which I have called invisible capital.

I do not appreciate the idyllic aspiration for a color-blind society; as a person of color, I'm somewhat fond of being seen. The same people who want us to believe that "they don't see color" are the same people who laugh when I respond, "I don't see age. Are you elderly, or a baby?"

We should accept difference simply for what it is—not as anything inherently good or bad. When we use differences such as race to separate one group from another instead of highlighting common ground, we create an impediment to success. In fact, we mix a highly toxic cocktail of homophily and propinquity.

So we can't ignore race, and we can't promote race as an effective solution for dealing with what Professor Michael Brown of the University of California, Santa Cruz, calls "durable racial inequality." What then should we do?

The goal should not be to simply choose between race-explicit and so-called "race-neutral" policy language and solutions, because the former are highly imperfect and the latter are impossible. The GI Bill was supposed to be a race-neutral piece of legislation that in reality actually expanded already wide gaps between White and Black veterans. Black World War II vets like my paternal grandfather got financial assistance to buy a home or go to school. However, as so many other Black veterans discovered, assistance without meaningful access was not real opportunity for advancement. Many Black GI Bill recipients got mortgage assistance from the government—

while restrictive covenants kept them from moving into newly built suburbs where only their White counterparts were welcomed with open arms.

The federal government would help pay for postsecondary education for returning GIs, but if the university denied you access because of your race, ethnicity, or religion, what good was that? The cumulative effect of these so-called race-neutral laws was to increase the rate at which invisible capital was acquired by one group at the expense of another. The haunting effects of that stockpiling of invisible capital can be seen two or three generations later, when today we see precipitous downward socioeconomic mobility among the groups who benefited the least from these programs—let alone the descendants of that generation who did not qualify for or could not take advantage of the GI Bill.[17] Residential segregation and other forms of structural inequality did not create invisible capital, but they certainly magnified its power exponentially.

Race-focused entrepreneurial policy solutions create as many problems as they were meant to solve. Who defines what race is and the extent to which it can evolve, as social identities always do over time and space? Is the percentage of ownership by non-Whites or women the best way to determine if a firm should be classified as a DBE? Is being a person of color or a woman enough to have you declared "disadvantaged" as it relates to entrepreneurial opportunity? Are such programs beneficial if a DBE is, for instance, owned by a person of color or woman but employs only White men or outsources its operations to workers in other countries?

The aims of sound entrepreneurial policy and the language we use to promote it must be centered on democratizing entrepreneurial opportunity based on social impact rather than social identity and on shared prosperity rather than individual wealth acquisition. We should be clearer about how and why we use the language and labels we invent. The most compelling reason we create categories in this field is that by so doing, we can actually build and work toward reaching proportional, but equalized, capacity within and between

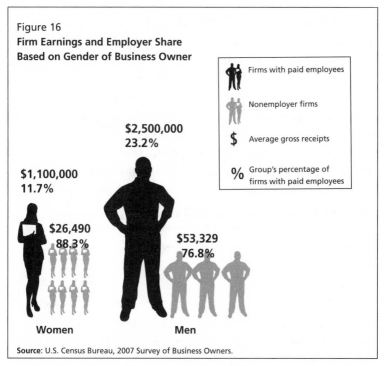

Figure 16
**Firm Earnings and Employer Share Based on Gender of Business Owner**

Firms with paid employees

Nonemployer firms

$ Average gross receipts

% Group's percentage of firms with paid employees

$2,500,000
23.2%

$1,100,000
11.7%

$26,490
88.3%

$53,329
76.8%

Women

Men

Source: U.S. Census Bureau, 2007 Survey of Business Owners.

communities. Much of that capacity-building can come from ac-knowledging and leveraging invisible capital to help level the play-ing field.

The answers here, though, are not nearly as important as the very real set of questions posed. And if there is still no consensus about these matters over forty years after these policies were instituted, that should signal that a public dialogue about these programs is long overdue. For too long, the question has been: Are these programs in fact constitutional? The larger question really must be: Are they use-ful based on how policymakers define success?

The best way to acquire invisible capital is to first make it visible. What we need is not color blindness, but a clear vision that acknowl-edges difference and understands the origins and impacts of those differences as we strive to achieve equality of opportunity. It is true that a rising tide lifts all boats. But whom does the rising tide benefit more—the swell behind the wheel of a yacht or the castaway hanging on to a piece of driftwood?

Too many well-intentioned set-aside programs falter because they blur outputs with outcomes and social conditions with the consequences of these conditions.

If programs have been set up to address existing patterns of discrimination, their aims must discretely counteract these forces. However, if we want programs that encourage broad inclusion, we must intentionally design them to address the effects of structural disparities. Further, over time those business owners labeled as disadvantaged will be able to build significant invisible capital themselves as a result of government and corporate procurement programs, thus creating intragroup gains to help level the playing field between groups.

## Community Impacts

The irony is that Democrats are usually the biggest promoters of such programs. And yet the underlying premise of many DBE set-aside programs is that they will result in a significant trickle-down effect—typically a Republican argument. The hope is that the success of those chosen few entrepreneurs with the greatest visible and invisible capital, and their anticipated largesse, will somehow reach the unwashed masses and help improve their collective lot in life.

The reality is different. A minuscule percentage of DBEs obtain government or large-scale corporate clients as a result of gaining access to this often incestuous and highly political world, and these opportunities have indeed increased the scale and profitability of their firms. These firms have also acquired additional invisible capital as a result of such contracts and will no doubt be able to leverage it in order to access still other opportunities. But there is no proof that their upward economic mobility has mitigated the enduring impact of the systemic disparities that these race- and gender-based programs were designed to overcome. Instead, programs that provide access to previously restricted business opportunities for disadvantaged business owners have done little more than create individual advantages for

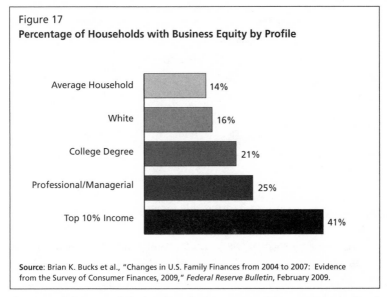

Figure 17
**Percentage of Households with Business Equity by Profile**

Average Household — 14%

White — 16%

College Degree — 21%

Professional/Managerial — 25%

Top 10% Income — 41%

**Source:** Brian K. Bucks et al., "Changes in U.S. Family Finances from 2004 to 2007: Evidence from the Survey of Consumer Finances, 2009," *Federal Reserve Bulletin*, February 2009.

their participants while leaving their communities as marginalized as ever.

The central defect in these policies is that they focus on *individuals* who come from designated communities rather than focusing their efforts on the communities themselves. Perhaps the best example of this latter approach is what I call the Clyburn Formula.

During the early debate on structuring a stimulus package to reinvigorate the U.S. economy during the Great Recession, Majority Whip Rep. James Clyburn (D-SC) suggested legislative language framed around three key numbers: 10-20-30. Rep. Clyburn's proposal was that at least 10 percent of federal stimulus funds should be directed, not to corporations, but to communities with poverty rates of at least 20 percent for at least thirty years.[18]

Congressman Clyburn was trying to fund new levees rather than just paying for more sandbags. His approach was not race based, it was solutions oriented. The problem his proposal addressed was not race-specific (although the consequences of the original disparities disproportionately impacted Blacks and Latinos, in particular). The problem was economic inequality, and the congressman's solution was too simple, too elegant—and was ultimately stripped from the final legislation. It was a legislative hand up—not a handout. It addressed the types of structural inequality that corporate media virtually never legitimate, yet represent one of our darkest (open) secrets: for most Americans the American Dream, as the late comedian George Carlin used to say, can be achieved only if you are asleep.

According to the American Dream Survey, conducted on behalf of Xavier University's Institute for Politics and the American Dream in February 2010:

- On a 1–10 scale measuring the current condition of the American Dream, nearly half of Americans rated the Dream lower than a "5" with nearly a quarter assigning the lowest possible rating. In contrast only 5% awarded the highest possible mark, a "10," and the total number of scores 7 or higher merely matched the number rating the Dream a "1." ...

- ... The Dream's legacy has also fallen into dangerous territory. Sixty percent of our respondents believe that it has become harder to reach the American Dream than it was for their parents' generation; only one-third feel it is easier. And an even greater majority 68% say that it will be harder still for their children to reach the Dream with a stunning 45% believing it will be much harder;

- ... amidst a very critical view of the Dream's current status, a consistent disparity in outlook between non-Whites and Whites, immigrants and native-born Americans. African-Americans, Latinos, and 1st or 2nd generation immigrants view the Dream more positively on nearly every measure in this survey than do White Americans. Or in other words, the part of our society that is still, by and large, worst off in terms of social or economic measurements, is also the same group that is most positive about the American Dream.[19]

## Incubators, Angels, and Unicorns

I believe in angels. No, not that kind of angel. I mean angel investors. In fact, I have benefited from angel investors in the past, and was quite thankful and honored to take their money. Angel investors are the folks some entrepreneurs and business owners approach about investing in their enterprises when they can't go to (or as is often the case, return to) their family, friends, and colleagues for money to help fund their ventures. The more jaded among us call this initial set of informal investors "F cubed": family, friends, and fools. (Harsh, I know.) But much of the initial capital raised by nascent entrepreneurs and business owners comes from people who invest in the proverbial jockey more than the horse (or the mule). They do so because they want to be supportive or may really believe that "it's so crazy it just might work" and want to be in on the ground floor of something big. Whatever the rationale, these are the people who get hit up first. Angel investors, for those who know they exist and can figure out how to access them, are often next in line—particularly if debt financing through a bank cannot be pursued for various reasons.[20]

The reality is that most people have never even heard of angel investors—or "angels," for short. Just knowing what this label stands for represents a component of invisible capital closely associated with cultural capital—perhaps growing up around entrepreneurs or being in professional or educational environments where this jargon became second nature to you. Familiarity with the term "angel" in and of itself may well correlate to a higher level of access to the networks that can lead you to them, irrespective of how smart, creative, or well-mannered you may be. And the cultural capital associated with such terminology and resources is also linked to wealth. After all, angel investors are almost by definition high-income individuals who are inclined to invest part of their disposable income in new ventures in return for a healthy yield on their high-risk infusion of capital.

Unlike venture capitalists who reinvest the funds of their investors into high-scale business ventures, angel investors invest their own money in businesses, either as individuals or as members of a semi-formal or formal group of angels. But even though most angel investors are not independently wealthy or sophisticated business people themselves, as is often suggested by members of the Entrepreneurial-Industrial Complex,[21] they might as well be unicorns to most business people who do not have (or know how to leverage) the invisible capital to ever approach them. If these same entrepreneurs are part of a well-resourced business incubator, however, the probability they can get access to such investors may be somewhat improved.

In many respects, business incubators are like charter schools. Seemingly everyone (outside of unionized teachers and highly degreed education experts, that is) believes they're the best thing since sliced bread. In their brief history in the United States, they've been so popular politically that both parties have embraced them like baseball, hot dogs, apple pie, and Chevrolet (which, of course, is the iconic American car model named after a Swiss man of the same name).

Just as "small business" is cherished alongside motherhood, business incubators are roundly hailed as important engines of entrepreneurship. However, like charter schools, they are a mixed bag. Charter schools with no science labs, gymnasiums, or teachers with more than two years of work experience: not so good. Incubators without well-trained staff, access to funding for their clients, or programmatic rigor? Equally shoddy.

Business incubators are entities that assist start-up ventures.[22] They do so in myriad ways and for a range of constituencies. Some incubators are set up as private nonprofits, while others are government-backed or university-based entities. Some are open to the public on a first-come, first-served basis, while others are open to specific groups—for example, single mothers, veterans, ex-offenders, culinary arts professionals, or university faculty and students.

With the right mix of training, capitalization, and networks, incubators have the potential to teach their clients and help build for them the invisible capital that nascent and would-be entrepreneurs so desperately need. Incubators that host business plan competitions but don't imbue in their clients the importance of invisible capital are like lifeguard training programs that allow their participants to graduate without learning how to swim. Affordable office space, shared administrative services, and "elevator pitch" trainings are invaluable, but incubators that provide content without context may very well be glorified cubicle farms with great PR.

As a former director of a nationally recognized urban business incubator, I know firsthand the opportunities they have to help their clients develop invisible capital as well as the challenges that incubators face. When I was the vice president of entrepreneurial programs at a nonprofit-based business assistance organization born out of an independent study conceived by Wharton MBA students, I was asked on occasion to be a judge for a business plan competition, a feature of the program mandated by its well-intentioned philanthropic funder.

The participants were all under twenty-five years old. Some were high school dropouts, while others had earned their GEDs. Some were attending or had received an associate's degree from the Community College of Philadelphia, and a few were students at the University of Pennsylvania or Drexel University.

Invariably, the winners of these business plan competitions were students from the more selective schools. Were they more entrepreneurially oriented than their counterparts? No. Were they harder working? No. Were they more business savvy? No. Were their ideas or business models more compelling than those of their less educated peers? Rarely. So why did students from elite schools always win these competitions? Two words: invisible capital.

The Penn and Drexel students were more adept at using technology. They could write better. They were better trained in conducting research. They were more confident speaking in front of audiences. Their projects were often connected to experiences they had had working in other professional or educational environments, and their plans incorporated how they would secure funding, talent, or customers based on their various social networks. They had more human, cultural, and social capital, not to mention economic capital. It wasn't even close.

The problem with these competitions, I soon realized, was that they did not rate the viability of the business model but the ability of the contestant to advocate for her venture in clear, substantive, and compelling ways. While this is important, it was not supposed to be the purpose of the competition, which was to reward the person with the best business plan, one that (at least in theory) would be related to the most viable business model. However, the contests always turned into a virtual beauty contest, where beauty was defined by eloquence, clarity of thought, poise, presentation, and the use of language often associated with conventional intelligence (aka cultural capital). Eliza Doolittle mimicked the patrician ladies, and in so doing, she was accepted as their peer regardless of her intellect, values, or skills. To them, Eliza's most important tacit skill was her ability to assimilate.

The winners of these business competitions walked away with a nominal prize, big smiles, and their egos stroked. The losers left with serious mixed lessons. First, many undoubtedly thought that their business concepts and models were inferior to those of the winners, without any indication why that was the case (when in fact it rarely was). Second, they did not know how influential their lack of invisible capital was in diminishing their chances of excelling, largely because they didn't even know that they were being judged (albeit unconsciously) on the amount of invisible capital they brought to the competition.

The participants who left without a prize needed a crash course in invisible capital. Only then would they know what next steps to take to improve their chances in the future. As it was, the winners likely thought they were more entrepreneurially gifted than their peers when in fact they were merely being rewarded for being good test-takers. Their less fortunate counterparts might very well have been more adept at entrepreneurship, but until they discovered and accessed the unseen forces that culminate in invisible capital, they were unsuspecting casualties of something they didn't even know they needed.

Too often, incubators simply imitate the SBA business plan competitions, dress-for-success seminars, elevator pitches, and PowerPoint trainings. These MBA-style techniques are not designed for entrepreneurs who have yet to understand or cultivate invisible capital. Moreover, many such programs do not adequately recognize the broad motivations nascent entrepreneurs have for undertaking a new venture. As the saying goes, when all you have is a hammer, everything looks like a nail.

Many incubators and entrepreneurship workshops and seminars are thus one-size-fits-all events that proselytize a kind of hollow achievement validated by the Entrepreneurial-Industrial Complex, but fail to address the nonmarket motivations of entrepreneurs, whose concepts of success and wealth are far more holistic than anything penned by Donald Trump's ghostwriters.

Many such entrepreneurship boosters presume that the only type of success worth having is a scalable business that can grow well past twenty employees. That's as much of a fantasy for most would-be entrepreneurs—particularly those with little invisible capital—as expecting to see a unicorn at your local zoo.

Instead, boosters in this capacity need to teach would-be and nascent entrepreneurs about the relevance and impact of invisible capital on their enterprises' chances of survivability, and teach this along with all the other key capabilities that every business owner should have. Incubator staff should assess the wide array of factors that indicate levels of invisible capital, from digital literacy to cultural competency, to breadth and depth of various social networks, to access and experience interacting with potential stakeholders, be they funders, vendors, potential partners, or future employees.

These questions are not sexy, but they are essential. Foundations must not be seduced by the romanticized (and nonthreatening) economic initiatives that promote self-reliance over empirical efficacy. Foundation program officers must be more rigorous with their investment in knowledge acquisition and funding of programs that truly foster just, inclusive, and sustainable enterprises that improve the communities they operate in. They must avoid falling into the trap of guilt- or nostalgia-based philanthropy that lowers performance and compliance standards for the sake of qualitatively dubious returns. The same applies to the private sector and to the local, state, and federal governments with which they must interact.

Along with increasing business owners' human capital, incubators can teach entrepreneurial literacy. They can explain to would-be business owners how to leverage their financial capital and how to use social networks to build business contacts. Many new entrepreneurs are afraid to ask their friends and family for money, or ask for too little. Incubators can give new nascent entrepreneurs a more practical sense of what their business needs to be viable and help them identify potential sources of that all-important start-up cash.

They can place prospective entrepreneurs in internships, apprenticeships, and mentorship programs. Since we know that two of the five predictors of entrepreneurial viability are working in a family-owned business and working in the industry you plan to enter, why can't we place entrepreneurs-in-training in these work situations for a period of six months, giving them critical experience and new networking opportunities?

All of these changes will help entrepreneurs. Perhaps the most important, however, will be redefining entrepreneurial success.

# 5

# Reframing Entrepreneurial Success ... and Failure

One night, after work, a woman came upon a neighbor who was hunched over, looking for something by a street lamp. She asked her neighbor what he was doing. He replied that he was looking for his keys. Naturally, she asked where he had lost them. He said, "Over there," pointing to a dark area beyond where he was scouring the well-lit asphalt. Puzzled, she asked, "So, why are you looking over here?" Unfazed, he answered, "Because this is where the light is."

This vignette is not unlike how most government agencies and other organizations assess entrepreneurial success. They look where the light is. What they see is facts and figures. So when you ask them how they hope to help entrepreneurs, they will answer that they promote entrepreneurship by "gauging and documenting the myriad factors that influence entrepreneurial participation and performance."

The problem is that the "myriad factors" these agencies find are the ones in the light. They miss the factors that are in the dark—the set of acquired and inherited assets that make up invisible capital. Without understanding the power of invisible capital, merely poring over raw data on entrepreneurship—let alone without context—would be about as useful as a one-legged man in an ass-kicking contest.

In fact, because invisible capital is so complex a phenomenon, I don't think it makes any sense to gauge factors and document figures. Instead, if someone asked me how I would broadly promote

**115**

entrepreneurial success, I would tell them to start by envisioning the desired outcome and work backwards.

First, I would want to know who is asking the question and why. Are they public officials, angel investors, journalists, or program officers at a regional foundation? Until we know who's inquiring and how they interpret their stake in the solution, it's all just theory. Second, I would want to know how they define "success" (or, as I like to ask my clients during initial consultations, "What does success look like?"). Last, who are the direct and indirect beneficiaries of this success?

Too often policyshapers (and the media that cover them) make the cavalier assumption that *all* business is *good* business; that new jobs are therefore good (and lasting) jobs; that entrepreneurship is meritocratic or inherently beneficial to our entire economy and the nation. (Anyone remember Enron?)

We can grouse all we want about Wall Street bankers, K Street lobbyists, and complacent career politicians, but the responsibility is squarely on our shoulders as citizens to reframe success, failure, and progress.

### The Bureaucracies We Deserve

I worked in government for a few years, first as a legislative aide in the U.S. Senate and then as a writer, researcher, and trainer for the White House Conference on Small Business, which worked closely with the SBA's Office of Advocacy. I learned a great deal about our federal government from the inside out.

In both of my positions in Washington, I was technically what is called a "political appointee." In other words, I was not a member of the civil service, more pejoratively referred to as the "bureaucrats" whose positions and vocational orientations are (in theory) nonpartisan. These are the often anonymous workers whom pandering politicians like to blame for just about everything. The reality is, however, many of them provide highly critical services to our nation and those who (ostensibly) represent us in Congress. Perhaps that's why there

was so much buzz around First Lady Michelle Obama when she visited several federal agencies in early 2009 just to thank the civil servants
so often caricatured by politicians and the public alike, but who rarely
garner any public praise when their efforts are exemplary.[1]

These government workers are sworn to political neutrality—professionally, that is. However, what they do in the service of civil society is directly influenced by the legislative and partisan agendas of the
political forces that dominate Capitol Hill, statehouses, county seats,
and city halls from coast to coast. Granted, no branch of government is beyond reproach, but numerous agencies provide functional
stability, continuity, and dispassionate and focused competency in a
public sector too often denigrated by the shortsighted grandstanding
of, and petty bickering between, elected officials. How the bureaucracies within these government agencies are staffed, funded, held
accountable (or not), and characterized by mainstream media is based
in no small part on the political calculations and dim-wittedness (or
brilliance) of members of Congress and the executive branch whose
agendas and priorities are highly influenced by us. You know: "We
the people!"

Sadly, many of our elected officials are elected to serve in roles that
should require a level of entrepreneurial literacy that they simply do
not have, nor may ever commit to acquiring. For many, the talking
points provided by their dutiful staffers make up what little they know
about the issues, drawn to a considerable extent from the concise but
thorough Cliff's Notes–style information packets generated by the
Congressional Research Service, and supplemented by ear candy that
serves the agendas of their most favored lobbyists, advocacy groups,
party officials, and influential constituents (read: donors).

The resultant entrepreneurial illiteracy in our nation's halls of
power would be laughable if it didn't have such disastrous effects.
Not only do many of our legislators and members of the press (in the
increasingly enfeebled realm that is the shrinking Fourth Estate) lack
the general baseline knowledge of entrepreneurship and commerce,
this unacceptable deficiency keeps them from adequately performing

c. How can you reasonably judge the industry, or community if you don't know the rules of the scoring system?

For the legislative staffers, civil servants, and researchers who pore over the terabytes of data compiled on this topic, the rules are not important. What matters most to them, I suspect, is their ability to access, synthesize, and format information in a timely and effective manner on behalf of their bosses. The point here is that at the end of the day, *we're* their bosses.

The fact that most of us forget this or pretend it's not our job to hold them accountable is at the very heart of why we remain so unaware of all the things within our grasp that could promote the kind of entrepreneurship that does more than just make the rich richer or fill our garage with newer, shinier versions of the ThighMaster.

Albert Einstein once wrote that "everything that counts can't be counted," but we nevertheless know that what our society chooses to measure is what our society values most. It's ironic that, in a nation whose founding document enshrines among the unalienable rights of its people the pursuit of happiness, not even NPR listeners are demanding the day's Happy Planet Index rating or other quality-of-life assessments; rather, they're listening for the frequent Dow reports that most Americans—irrespective of formal education—are probably not financially sophisticated enough to comprehend.

The goal here, however, is not to boycott NPR nor to pledge to bone up on Wall Street jargon. Rather, our challenge is to be mindful of what we're being told, analyze its content (and intent), and work collectively to set a higher, more robust standard for what passes for entrepreneurial advocacy and reportage.

I'm no animal rights activist, but I know that "hugging a puppy every morning" probably doesn't meaningfully address or correct animal endangerment. But that's essentially what our elected officials and most Entrepreneurial-Industrial Complex adherents are telling us to do when they say things like "We need to lower taxes so that our citizens can keep their hard-earned dollars so they can invest it or start new businesses." From Barack Obama to Newt Gingrich, the EIC has a hold on our minds and on our mouths. So, when you hear dreck like that in the twenty-four-hour news cycle, think of the puppy dog.

I like puppy dogs as much as the next person, but not enough to be distracted from the inconvenient truth that as a citizenry we are some of the least taxed people of any industrialized nation—especially our wealthiest citizens. It's not taxes that are thwarting the creation of new, viable enterprises in this country.[2] It's invisible capital (which you may not have enough of or are not properly leveraging) that is limiting our economic potential for shared prosperity.

In the next section, you will see how much of what we need to know about the way invisible capital functions is already being studied by our government and academic institutions. However, public and private entities aren't "playing well with others," as it were. They're not talking to each other as much or as well as they could or should. Moreover, they are not making their findings as accessible as they need to be—one of the reasons I wrote this book.

And now that you know why invisible capital must be understood and systematically leveraged, let's take a look at how this can happen right now—no legislation necessary!

## Positive Business Outcomes (aka "Success") by the Numbers

According to economists, policy wonks, and academic researchers, there are four universally accepted measures of positive business outcomes (aka "success"):

- Revenues (gross receipts)
- Profits (net earnings)
- Payroll (number of paid employees)
- Longevity (survival rate)

Not surprisingly, these metrics value growth and profitability over all else. They are neither new, nor particularly creative, measures of business viability or success. However, they offer a good starting point for baseline organizational progress. Plenty of data on these measures is gathered, compiled, and analyzed. But these four factors only tell us about businesses that already exist rather than entrepreneurial ventures in their infancy.

There are, of course, numerous studies that never see the light of day outside of esoteric academic conferences and journals. And even if they were broadly available to the general public, they would be virtually unintelligible because of their dense jargon and theory, as well as prohibitively expensive for the average nascent entrepreneur or otherwise curious reader. Beyond the fact that these academic and governmental tomes can cure insomnia, many such publications contain treasure troves of information that may dispel many far-fetched and baseless claims about how and why certain business owners excel and why others don't.

One such academic book worth reading is the groundbreaking *Race and Entrepreneurial Success: Black-, Asian- and White-Owned Businesses in the United States*, written by entrepreneurial researchers Alicia Robb and Robert Fairlie. They have identified five key predictors of entrepreneurial viability across the board:

The industry in which entrepreneurs choose to launch their ventures;
Their previous work experience in a family-owned business;
Their previous work experience in a business that sold products or services similar to their new enterprise;
• The founders' level of educational attainment; and
• Access to sufficient start-up capital.[3]

Conducted by the U.S. Census Bureau, the Characteristics of Business Owners (CBO) is the largest data set on U.S. business owners in the country. It contains exhaustive information about business owners based on a raft of demographic and psychographic questions that have been seen and culled by only a few researchers. I'm thankful that Professors Robb and Fairlie had the determination, vision, and ability to access and painstakingly analyze this massive amount of

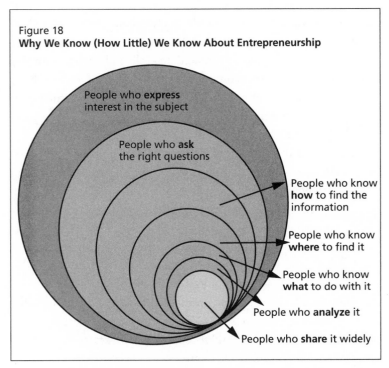

Figure 18
Why We Know (How Little) We Know About Entrepreneurship

People who express interest in the subject

People who ask the right questions

People who know how to find the information

People who know where to find it

People who know what to do with it

People who analyze it

People who share it widely

microdata, but their capacity to do so perfectly illustrates why this entrepreneur-obsessive culture has yet to expand the general public's knowledge about this vital subculture and economic engine.

Although a number of interested parties have sought access to this treasure trove of government data on U.S. entrepreneurial activity, only a handful of researchers have actually been granted access.[4] We don't have the requisite knowledge about entrepreneurship because the information pulled from the data collected rarely sees the light of day, nor is it made accessible to people without PhDs. Don't get me wrong—some of my best friends have PhDs, and I'm very impressed with them. But this fact does not help expose invisible capital or help combat the Entrepreneurial-Industrial Complex. We may know what (little) we know, but there's still far too much we don't know that we don't know. In fact, what we don't know can (and likely does) fill an entire federal office building in Washington, housing mountains of data, waiting to be meaningfully analyzed and converted to real, usable information on which sound and innovative civic, academic, and private initiatives should be based. Literally millions of would-be, new, and existing business owners and their advocates are needlessly functioning under long outdated, if not entirely faulty, assumptions about the entrepreneurial landscape.

So how do these factors individually and collectively relate to invisible capital and their role in increasing entrepreneurial opportunity? First, they demonstrate that inequality is built in from the start of any entrepreneurial venture, because some entrepreneurs come from wealth or highly influential social and professional networks, and others do not. Timely access to *sufficient* start-up funds, as previously alluded to, is one of the most important determinants linked to positive business outcomes.

But start-up capital, in and of itself, is neither mammon nor manna from heaven. Money is not the only factor that has a significant influence on business outcomes. The other factors are connected at least in part to human, cultural, and social capital—that is, to *achieved* factors that the entrepreneur *can* control.

Educational attainment begins with the elementary school you attend, a factor you cannot control. However, even as an adult, you can recast the die, working your way through community college to a four-year college and a bachelor's degree. Formal education is cultural capital that comes easier for those born to highly educated and wealthy families, but it is highly attainable by all.

Likewise, *relevant* work experience is a type of human capital. You are one step ahead if your family owns a business that you may have been "voluntold" to work in as a teenager (or even younger). You are also a step ahead if the kind of work and study that you were raised to value leads to a high-income or high-prestige career choice. Not surprisingly, such careers strongly correlate to industries in which highly scalable ventures abound, such as information technology. Certainly, a strong work ethic is virtually irreplaceable, but conventional entrepreneurial success stemming from leveraging one's skills in typewriter repair may not bode as well for building a large-scale entrepreneurial pursuit as tapping into one's training as an engineer in the field of nanotechnology.

However, once this kind of capital becomes visible—that is, once you realize you should get work experience in a family-owned business and in a business similar to your prospective venture—you can go about applying for those kinds of positions. Of course, whether you can get those positions may also depend to some degree on *ascribed* values—your native tongue, race, gender, and so forth.

All of these factors seem relatively straightforward. What does it mean, however, to make a successful choice of venture? To answer that question, we first have to reevaluate success.

## Reevaluating Success

These studies examine factors for business success: *factors*, not guarantees. However, they do not question how conventional success is defined, and how our current very limited definition impacts industries, local economies, natural environments, cultural communities, or civil society. This is not an indictment of the civil servants who are responsible for collecting data and issuing these reports. It is merely a statement of fact: they are often underfunded, understaffed, and under pressure by their politically appointed bosses to conduct themselves in ways that produce more heat than light.

The onus is on policymakers and an engaged citizenry to demand that these frames of broad sustainability are explicitly defined, and accounted for, by the bureaucracies we empower to crunch the numbers on our behalf. After all, what's the point of all of these studies, surveys, and reports if they don't further the lofty missions cited on these agencies' websites? More important, what good is the information if it can't be readily used to bolster our economy and strengthen our democracy—particularly if people don't know this information exists?

As the old story cited at the beginning of this chapter illustrates, people tend to look for things where there's the most light—or interest, public debate, or preexisting data—even if those places are not the best or most relevant sites of information. The Entrepreneurial-Industrial Complex generates a lot of light (and exponentially more heat) with the myth-based rhetoric and complementary merchandising it seeks to palm off on the world. And truth, justice, and equity are mere buzzwords to some of the complex's most ideologically driven and mindless profit-hounds.

In doing research for this book, I scoured countless academic books, government reports, and think tank–sponsored studies. I have yet to meet a person in business who is familiar with any one of them. The same goes for the influential entrepreneurship advocates I know who are public servants, civic leaders, community development–focused program directors at foundations, and so on. Like invisible capital, much of the information we could benefit from is hidden in plain view or between the covers of $150 books.

Critical information is processed by such bureaucracies as the Federal Reserve, the Department of Labor, the Department of Commerce, the Treasury Department, the U.S. Census Bureau, and so on. If you Google long enough, you will eventually find most of these sources. But it's not easy. It's because it is so difficult to find (and understand) this information that most people think running a business may not be as hard as it truly is.

Let's drill down into one of the five key predictors of entrepreneurial viability, the choice of industry. Again, we'll turn to a story to illustrate the difference the choice of venture makes.

Joan and Jim are first cousins. They grew up in the same middle-class suburb of Minneapolis. Their grandfather started a weekly newspaper back in the 1940s that by the time they were born had grown significantly and was acquired by a national newspaper chain. Joan and Jim were the only entrepreneurially minded grandchildren of the larger group of beneficiaries of the estate. The bequest afforded them each a handsome inheritance—$75,000—that provided them with a lump sum of money that most Americans would never have any at one time, let alone at the underripe age of eighteen.

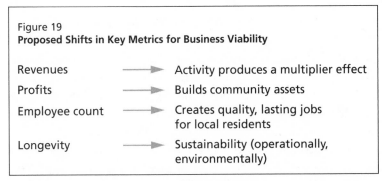

Figure 19
**Proposed Shifts in Key Metrics for Business Viability**

Revenues ⟶ Activity produces a multiplier effect

Profits ⟶ Builds community assets

Employee count ⟶ Creates quality, lasting jobs
for local residents

Longevity ⟶ Sustainability (operationally,
environmentally)

Joan chose to use this money to pay for college and thereby avoided having to take out the loans that most of her friends and classmates were saddled with. Jim decided to bypass college altogether and use his inheritance to start an online advertising business. Joan's entrepreneurial thirst was quenched by starting a tutoring service geared to local high school students and their parents who wanted to improve their chances of being accepted by selective colleges.

Both Joan and Jim made a choice of industry based on their personal interests. For both, their goal was economic sustainability. Jim's choice of venture, however, also provides room for growth. His online advertising company, if well run, could expand considerably. Joan's tutoring service is likely to stay small, because it requires knowledgeable staff and no doubt a certain amount of personal hand-holding of parents and students.

Let's assume both ventures grow, a real accomplishment given the statistics cited in chapters 1 and 2. In five years, Jim's company has grown to twenty part-time workers based in Bangalore, India, and is being courted by Yahoo! Joan has added a part-time administrative assistant and two other part-time tutors from the mixed-income neighborhood where she was raised. Which of these companies is a success?

The experts will examine the cousins' five factors and tell you that in three key metrics—sales, profits, employees—Jim's company bests Joan's. Like a disproportionate number of women in business, Joan chose an entrepreneurial endeavor that was not high-growth in terms of revenues or employee count.[5] But ask Joan, and she may tell you that she made a conscious choice to do so because quality of life—particularly having a flexible schedule—and hiring local talent were more important to her than running a fast-growing company.

Author and prolific entrepreneurship scholar Scott A. Shane points out that Joan is not alone: "While such topsy-turvy priorities are anathema to the major industrial players in the post–World War II American economy, increasingly growth for growth's sake, which stresses market share and profit maximization, it is a trend among the growing ranks of even the most entrepreneurial of the unincorporated self-employed."[6] Some entrepreneurs are looking for economic sustainability and quality of life, rather than meeting some agencies' arbitrary metrics.

When it comes to contextualizing why many more female business owners choose "lifestyle" ventures, "flexibility" and "quality of life" issues merit greater scrutiny. For example, when researchers from the University of Michigan analyzed data from the Panel Study of Income Dynamics, they found that married women with children did *far* more housework than their male counterparts. Moreover, single men of all ages did more housework than their married brethren.[7] Perhaps these are not stunning revelations to most women (or divorced people). But the takeaway here is that nascent entrepreneurs do not make their decisions in a vacuum, but in the real world, where it matters who has what form of invisible capital. In the above scenario, the way in which gender and marital status intersect can either be a significant asset or liability.

Let's look at some more examples:

Bob started a home-based computer repair shop in Billings, Montana. He runs it as a sole proprietorship. Bob's business required little start-up capital, but it's also not likely to sell shares in the stock market or receive bailout money because it may one day be "too big to fail."

Bob's brother, Bill, went to college, became a scientist, and founded a nanotechnology firm based on multiple patents. He set it up as a limited liability company and has received his first round of venture capital. It may be quite profitable in time and highly scalable in terms of employment size and revenues. Both these companies were started by a single owner. Both these entrepreneurs are hardworking. Both chose to pursue an entrepreneurial path to leverage their technical competencies. But these two paths could not be farther apart. Bob is essentially a member of the growing ranks of the "unincorporated self-employed." Bill's firm is among the less than 3 percent of U.S. firms that owns intellectual property such as trademarks, copyrights, and patents, and the significantly less than 1 percent that successfully secure institutional equity investments in the form of venture capital financing. In fact, according to the National Venture Capital Association, only about 3,200 companies received venture capital funding in 2007.[8] That's just higher than a 1 in 1,000 chance of securing this type of investment, assuming each year about 2 million start-ups are established in the U.S. alone.

Are both firms equally successful? Again, how do we measure success? By all the metrics, Bill's nanotechnology company is far more successful than Bob's repair shop. Yet let's also look at what impact these businesses have on the community. Bill's exciting venture may produce a whole new technology—or it may fold, or it may make one element of one process slightly more productive. Bob's shop helps the local business people in his community who rely on computers for their business; he helps seniors who may use their computers to keep in touch with relatives; he helps busy families whose kids need computers for their homework. Bob is making a substantial contribution to his community. Who is to say his business is not a success?

## ... And Failure

Just as we should not always rely on data-based metrics to make assumptions about business success, we should be careful about how we define business failures (also referred to in government parlance as "terminations" or "closures"). The following three examples give us a look at businesses that fail by the numbers:

James was a first-time entrepreneur. His foray into business wasn't pretty. The result: maxed-out credit cards, a bad breakup with his live-in partner, five years out of the conventional workforce, and thousands of work-hours of invaluable entrepreneurial experience in how *not* to run a start-up venture.

Maybe James, despite his various setbacks, saw the glass as half full—particularly if he realized he was going to be a serial entrepreneur. (His live-in partner, however, thought that James's business was a complete and utter failure.) James knew that his missteps and misadventures in business thus far would only make him better prepared for his next venture. Whether he was aware of it consciously or not, he knew that he had acquired invaluable knowledge, skills, resources, and networks over the past five years—invisible capital that could greatly improve his entrepreneurial viability the next time around.

Hank, Sanjay, and Chip went to college together and became friends as fellow engineering students. After graduating, they started a software engineering firm based on an innovation developed during a class project the three had worked on their senior year. Their business faltered for various reasons, but the infamous tech slide of the spring of 2000 surely didn't help. Before they shut down operations, however, they filed for a U.S. utility patent related to their flagship technology. They almost forgot about the application amid the dissolution of their start-up enterprise. However, a few months after they all moved on to other things, their patent was granted and they eventually sold it for several million dollars. Their business died, but the fruits of their labor were harvested in an unanticipated but highly lucrative manner.

Should the termination of their business be considered a failure? Nope.

Mary had a little laminating business. Actually, it was little when she inherited it from her uncles, but under her leadership it has consistently grown in terms of revenues and employment. Mary was the fourth-generation descendant of the founder of a nearly century-old, family-owned firm that had been only marginally profitable even during its golden era. In recent years, though, the business had fallen on hard times. Many of her direct competitors had gone out of business or had been acquired by regional market leaders. She did all she could to keep the firm viable by making broad innovations and adopting creative management and financing approaches, but to no avail.

After years of rebuffing the offers of her industry's regional market leader, Mary finally acquiesced and, with the approval of her board of directors, sold her great-grandfather's company to a much larger corporation that agreed to retain 80 percent of her employees, people whom she and her stock-owning relatives considered extended family. The firm would be absorbed into the larger business, but its ongoing operations would no longer bear the family name or its brand.

Was this business closure a failure? To Mary, maybe. To her former employees whose jobs she fought to keep post-acquisition, probably not. (To Mary's relatives who were sitting on the sidelines with no stock, absolutely.)

The often-vaunted entrepreneurial travails of the elite Silicon Valley cohort are emblematic of the kind of entrepreneurial culture that values failure not only as an accepted part of business life, but an expected and highly valued precondition for greater opportunity and professional insight. (Of course, if the financial and professional downsides of shutting down a new venture do not irreparably hurt one's financial net worth or tamper with one's safety net or job prospects, it's far easier to be philosophical about the benefits of "failure.")

Business closures should not be equated with business failures. The former status is factual, while the latter is subjective. We must not only understand the definitions surrounding entrepreneurship, but also appreciate the influence of the terminology itself on how we interpret and value the role of the entrepreneurial sector and its impact on our national economy and our society—particularly when the entrepreneurs who make this sector hum are sitting across from us at the dinner table or staring back at us in the mirror.

## Nonfarm, Nonprofit, and the Status Quo

Entrepreneurship has to be more inclusive of nontraditional organizations. Ultimately, if the enterprise innovates and engages in sustained economic activity in a context of some uncertainty, then, on some level, it is an entrepreneurial venture. Farms that grow organic food in rural communities that border urban centers where growers sell their produce need not be unduly excluded from federal data collection (or policy consideration) just because they are agricultural entities. The same is true for nonprofit organizations that create jobs and generate revenues based on needed services that help local or regional communities.

Success, therefore, deserves a broader governmental definition that is clearly aligned with communal sustainability and prosperity rather than mere economic growth. As the nonprofit organization Redefining Progress rightly points out, technically speaking, GDP doubly rewards certain broadly agreed-upon societal ills—for example, pollution and crime—based on how it accounts for the economic activity that produces these activities as well as the resulting work necessary to remediate their impacts.[9]

How, then, do we evaluate entrepreneurial success? Success in popular culture means creating a viable business that allows you to achieve the American Dream. It means building an enterprise in which you have amassed a lot of personal wealth and using that wealth to do whatever you want. It's about individual, material accomplishment. That's the narrative. The criteria are money and things.

But we have the ability to recast how we view success. Success should be based not just on achieving something for our personal ends, but creating an enterprise that benefits society at large. Most businesses serve local communities. If you can be prosperous and in the process help your community, whether by providing living-wage jobs, improving the environment, or simply supplying a needed service, that should define success.

Why should success be defined communally? Think about your business as you would your home. If all the houses in your neighborhood are being foreclosed and your biggest asset is your home, then you have to think communally. The positions of your neighbors impact you, and if they are failing you are hurt as well. The same is true of business. A business that benefits the community also benefits the entrepreneur.

The good news is that if you understand what the obstacles are, you're more likely to see the new opportunities that arise from acquiring this new insight, thereby significantly increasing your business viability. Understanding the more nuanced, nonclichéd meaning of community is one such pathway to improved business performance.

It goes well beyond venturing down this path just because it's "in" these days to talk about community. We need to promote community-centered enterprises because how we identify community—and the reciprocal value between the community and one's enterprise— may reveal strategic processes and structures that will improve your firm's sustainability.

Sustainability is a good thing—particularly if it can radiate broadly beyond yourself and your own affairs.

# 6

# Toward Commonwealth Entrepreneurship

As Americans we find ourselves, even with our rich resources, and high prosperity, unable to understand the chronic unemployment that still besets us, the need for greater education, health, and welfare services, and the fact that there do exist islands of poverty in our sea of affluence.... Inevitably, we are coming to appreciate that there must be a place in our schemes of things for those great intangible human values that cannot be represented on graphs or ledgers. We can no longer gauge our progress solely by the output of machines or the inflow of profits.... Creative community living becomes a reality only when each individual in that community, from birth to death, has an opportunity to achieve his maximum potential.

Whitney Young Jr., *To Be Equal* (1964)

In the fall of 2009, I ran into a woman whom I had not seen in some years. She was the daughter of one of the earliest and most enduring figures in my life: Mrs. Hilda Branch Thornton. Over the course of several decades, Mrs. Thornton helped nurture, train, and educate hundreds of Chicago children who attended her Lake Meadows Daycare. It was there that my intellectual curiosity was engaged, my creativity nurtured, and my social graces formed in ways that complemented what my parents and elders instilled in my brother and me.

Mrs. Thornton became an indelible image and symbol to me of what excellence, learning, and communal love felt like. So, as you can imagine, I choked up when her daughter reintroduced herself to me and informed me that her mother had recently died at the ripe age of ninety-six. As we talked, we traded the usual information about ourselves, and I told her about the work I was doing on this book. When I finished, Mrs. Thornton's daughter looked at me and said, "I guess my mother was an entrepreneur, huh?"

Here I was, the guy obsessed with entrepreneurship. In all my years reflecting on the beauty and value of my experience at that day care center, I had never once thought of it as a business, nor of my parents as customers or clients. Mrs. Thornton's business acumen had been invisible to me. But entrepreneurial she was, innovative and able to seize the opportunities available in her community. Her day care may not have created the "phantom wealth" of a Bear Stearns,[1] but she created a kind of wealth that to my way of thinking has far more value—her day care made the world just a little bit better for everyone.

Unfortunately, like so many ventures, Mrs. Thornton's enterprise is no more, but her legacy lives on in the guidance, love, and inspiration she offered to generations of children and their parents. This is one form of intangible, but no less valuable, communal wealth. When we ask what makes an enterprise a success, *social value* should be one of our answers. When we look to encourage the creation of new enterprises, or seek to make current enterprises viable, one of the marks on our yardstick must indicate whether this enterprise supports communal well-being. Prosperity that benefits a broad constituency is the type of business outcome we need to value more in this society. For it is this type of civic prosperity that sustains communities and the people who make them worth living in.

Neighborhoods, the physical embodiment of geographical communities, as John McKnight and Peter Block put it in their book *The Abundant Community*, require seven indispensable things that government, professions, and, yes, businesses alone cannot provide. They are: safety and security, health, the well-being of children, the environment and the land, an enterprising economy, food, and care.[2]

Free market proponents will claim that the creation of monetary value itself yields public good. Of course, there is public good in the creation of good jobs and vital services not provided by the public or independent sectors. Yet value creation should never be reduced to mere market value, nor trump shared values that transcend markets and embolden communities (versus simply catering to material consumption). No example of this distinction is clearer than the one referenced by the public policy think tank Redefining Progress, which began its 2006 *Genuine Progress Indicator* report by commenting on a wire service story:

**GDP muscles through**
Economy brushes off storms and expands by 3.8 percent in 3Q, beating estimates.
   The U.S. economy shook off headwinds from hurricanes Katrina and Rita to grow at a faster-than-expected 3.8 percent annual rate in the third quarter, a Commerce Department report showed Friday. (Reuters, 2005)
   Perhaps no headline in recent history does a better job of illustrating why our nation's most trusted measure of economic performance is so woefully out of sync with people's everyday experiences. In one fell swoop, these headlines dismissed the inequitable and catastrophic toll associated with 1,836 preventable deaths, over 850,000 housing units damaged, destroyed, or left uninhabitable, disruption of 600,000 jobs, permanent inundations of 18 square miles of marshland, destruction of 1.3 million acres of forest, and contamination caused by millions of gallons of floodwaters tainted by sewage, oil, heavy metals, pesticides, and other toxins as irrelevant to the U.S. economy.[3]

We are far from being the stakeholder society envisioned by Bruce Ackerman and Anne Alstott in their provocative book *The Stakeholder Society*. In some ways we have adopted a strategy that is the reverse of what Ackerman and Alstott suggest in that book.[4] Instead of (or in addition to) back-loading redress of inequalities, their plan confronts the uneven playing field from birth by creating $80,000 savings accounts that could be accessed only at age eighteen or after and used for such things as education and homeownership, investments, and (unadvisedly) starting a business.

Ackerman and Alstott's proposal would encourage life planning, since every citizen would have the ability to invest in their future in ways that would also benefit our economy and society at large.

We are a nation far too influenced by the myopia and deceptions of the Entrepreneurial-Industrial Complex, deceptions that unduly distract us from the value of the millions of important microenterprises—those firms that employ fewer than, say, ten workers. Most of them cater to local markets and are run by families earning less than their fully employed, salaried counterparts. Such often overlooked, underrepresented, and struggling businesses are not necessarily the economic backbone of our country they used to be, before Wall Street devoured our economy, but these small-scale, overwhelmingly neighborhood-based enterprises are important, too—particularly if they help build community wealth.

For local business owners like Mrs. Thornton, their work is a calling that transcends profit. I don't mean to glamorize the life of a mom-and-pop grocery store owner, or to generalize about the inherent goodness of the average business owner. I don't profess to know what lies in the hearts of millions of business owners from Seattle to Savannah. Rather, I am suggesting that not everyone who runs a business or seeks to establish an entrepreneurial venture is motivated primarily or exclusively by profit. People who go into business usually hope to make a profit. Practically speaking, however, few will ever achieve a significant level of profitability. According to the 2008 Kauffman Firm Survey, only 36 percent of businesses that made it to their fourth year earned revenues of $25,000 or more.[5]

Many entrepreneurs struggling to build viable businesses started their ventures as much out of a personal passion as a pursuit of profit. They seek to provide financial security for themselves and their families. They seek to convert a concept into a fully operational enterprise. They undertake a daunting odyssey toward innovating products, services, or processes that directly or indirectly improve the lives, livelihoods, or entire lifestyles of others, if not an entire population. These entrepreneurs are mission driven, and their businesses are led by values—values that dutifully acknowledge and embrace nonmarket forces. The goals of these entrepreneurs overlap with the public good. It is these entrepreneurs we must help the most, and with the most ingenuity. To do so, we must first bring invisible capital into the daylight. We must understand what constitutes entrepreneurial success and then create truly democratic opportunities for that success.

Not having considerable invisible capital keeps individuals and groups from fully participating in the otherwise vibrant entrepreneurial sector of our economy. But more important, hoarding invisible capital hobbles our nation by throttling its true potential to become the economically, environmentally, and socially sustainable society in which we all deserve to have equal footing to pursue happiness however we choose to define it.

Contrary to the meme of the American Dream, entrepreneurs can't make it alone. Entrepreneurs require significant networks of support. It is up to us, from community to community, to support entrepreneurs who will work for the public good or "the commons," as advocated for most recently by political scientist Elinor Ostrom, newly awarded Nobel Prize winner.[6] If we believe in democracy and equal opportunity, embrace entrepreneurship, and want continued prosperity for our nation, this prosperity must be shared in part through *commonwealth entrepreneurship*. We must cast aside Horatio Alger mythology and use our dynamic ingenuity as a nation to address the problems stemming from inequality in creative and morally consistent ways within political, economic, and social realms.

### The Value of "Small Business"

"Small Business America" is sacrosanct. To besmirch this noble sector of our economy and popular culture is to defame all that is holy in this great Land of Possibility. That said, allow me to say this: Small Business America is only as good as it serves in some real way *all* Americans.

The term "small business" is used in the same way as "family farm." We venerate family farms. They represent our country's agricultural roots. They epitomize our work ethic, our self-reliance, and our lauded autonomy. Yet most of the food we eat is neither grown locally nor harvested at the hands of such farmers. We exalt family farmers, but we fill our bellies with genetically modified "food" from their corporate behemoth rivals.

We love Small Business America, but we're afraid to look at the bottoms of all the items we buy at Walmart and see the ubiquitous "Made in China" sticker. If we truly care about the American economy, we need to end this hypocrisy and become more intentional about the types of businesses we patronize and advocate for—and make explicit our reasons for doing so.

In a world economy with multinational conglomerates spanning the globe, what does it mean to "Buy American" if a company's workforce is based in China or India or Mexico? Why should we support "small businesses" that discriminate against gay or female employees, dump toxins in our rivers, or sell defective merchandise to their customers? Small is not inherently good, nor does big always have to be bad.

What are the standards we must set for ourselves, our society, and the business community regarding what we hold most dear to the general welfare of our citizenry?

The solution is not just to replace "small business" and "family farm" with new memes like "community" and "Main Street." Innumerable Main Streets that bisected communities all across America were infected by Jim Crow in the past, and they have not necessarily transcended many other "isms" in the present. If it was difficult being a person of color, gay, or an independent woman on Main Street not so long ago, imagine how difficult it would have been to open a business on Main Street when invisible capital was that much more important despite being far less acknowledged.

The solution is not simply to tout businesses that create "good jobs at home." The fact is, not all "good jobs" are created equal. Just as not all jobs are good, not all growth is good. If all we are doing is creating economic growth for growth's sake, then we will not have learned our lesson from the Great Recession. Even the creator of the gross domestic product (GDP) formula, Simon Kuznets, said in 1934, "The welfare of a nation can scarcely be inferred from a measurement of national income,"[7] and it is thus an inadequate gauge for economic health. Moreover, growth for growth's sake has no demonstrable record of equitably expanding prosperity, and it likely never will.

What we need to do is adopt a new understanding of the American economy. We need to replace our dream of "more" with the maxim "Enough is good enough." "More" has been our mantra for the past sixty years, because ostensibly *more* is good. "More" is synonymous with prosperity and ingenuity—and that is the essence of the American Dream, because we are not satisfied with just having a good quality of life—we've defined success as having *more* than what your parents had. Besides, such economic growth lifts all boats, right?

In a word, no.

## Social Entrepreneurship Beyond Green Consumerism

By and large, Americans are no happier today than we were in 1961, when life satisfaction surveys were first conducted here and abroad. Income and wealth inequality between the rich and poor, White and "non-White," is in fact greater now than at any time in the twentieth century, as statistics elsewhere in this book have confirmed. We have been ravaged by the plague that is aptly labeled "affluenza,"[8] the highly contagious disease of gratuitous materialism and enormous wealth. We are working longer, despite stagnating wages and ever-increasing expenses for housing, utilities, food, education, and health care.

Figure 20
**Innovative Commonwealth Enterprise Structures**

- Community development financial institutions (CDFIs)
- Community development corporations (CDCs)
- Worker, producer, and consumer cooperatives
- Employee stock ownership programs (ESOPs)
- For-profit subsidiaries of nonprofit firms
- Low-profit limited liability companies (L3Cs)
- Benefit corporations (B Corps)
- Community land trusts (CLTs)
- Municipally owned corporations
- Social franchises
- Credit unions

For more information on these structures, visit www.InvisibleCapital.com.

We've been duped into believing that the Dow, GDP, and the Standard & Poor's 500 Index mean more than they really do. For most Americans, a far more comprehensive metric such as the Happy Planet Index would be unheard of or laughed off as a quixotic, tree-hugging fad, despite being recognized as a legitimate indicator for broad economic progress by several industrialized nations. (HPI is the three-pronged metric of the interplay of life satisfaction, life expectancy, and the ecological footprint of a given nation's populace.)[9]

We need to groom and sustain entrepreneurs who help us improve our HPI and other socioeconomic indices of communal well-being such as the Genuine Progress Index, a far more complex algorithm, many of whose variables are used to determine GDP.[10]

But as economist Jessica Gordon Nembhard points out, there is other "people-centered local economic development that is community-based and controlled, collaborative, democratically (or at least broadly) owned and governed through a variety of structures." Nembhard's list includes worker-, producer-, and consumer-owned cooperatives; community land trusts; employee stock ownership programs (ESOPs); collective not-for-profit organizations; municipally owned enterprises; community development financial institutions and credit unions; and community-controlled community development corporations (CDCs).[11]

Mutual aid associations and various other forms of cooperatives have existed for centuries in this country. They have been embraced in both urban and rural areas, from the Reconstruction-era South to the digital-era Pacific Northwest. Today, it's easier than ever to set up this kind of enterprise.

To those who think of enterprises only as profit-generating machines, these kinds of entities may not seem entrepreneurial. However, there is no reason that enterprises must be limited to for-profit concerns. Entrepreneurship is a process—a practice—not a destination or genetic predisposition. Its shape and value can be dictated by the opportunities we create. Some entrepreneurs will create great material wealth; others will create expansive employment, long-term technological advances, or rapid environmental remediation. Some will simply be good neighbors and promote what authors Ed Diener and Robert Biswas-Diener call "psychological wealth" that fosters the well-being we all seek, as enshrined in Jefferson's indelible phrase "life, liberty, and the pursuit of happiness."[12]

Structures for successful enterprises that can score high on the HPI are almost as varied as the products or services these entities sell. Some enterprises are built with the inherent capacity to grow quickly to address market demands and create significant value in the marketplace while providing social returns as well. These social enterprises benefit society by addressing deficiencies in the marketplace, such as the lack of a quality product or service that improves the lives of not only consumers in a given market, but the community in which that market functions. The most effective social enterprises thus create community assets beyond good products, good services, and good jobs. Other kinds of social enterprises we must invest in are those that have all the more resonance in the wake of the Great Recession.

Increasingly during severe economic downturns, we are forced to ask ourselves such previously unthinkable questions as: Do we need a domestic auto industry? Can we do away with an entire industry, like health insurance or offshore drilling? Can we wean ourselves off coal in the foreseeable future? There are many ways to address these questions, but the enterprises that address them in a way that benefits the commonwealth will retrain workers, address the needs of community stakeholders, and offer more environmentally responsible processes and products.

We live in a fragile democracy influenced in no small part by an evolving, post-meltdown economy. It is a consumer-oriented, growth-based economy whose evolution (or devolution) in recent decades has not provided significant improvements in quality of life, upward mobility, or democracy.

We have a hybrid economy that embraces entrepreneurship, but is overrun by industries that are all but monopolized by a few bloated conglomerates. Our history of invention and our entrepreneurial culture venerate inventors and small business owners. Yet we have not found an innovative way to fuse democracy with entrepreneurship.

We espouse the aphorism "A rising tide lifts all boats." Yet our collective greed and individualistic materialism have steadily eroded long-held respect for community and institutions built to protect, and advocate for, the public good.

Commonwealth entrepreneurship is not just another name for social entrepreneurship. It certainly overlaps with it, but it goes even deeper. At its core is the blending of innovation and the creation of community assets that themselves foster greater capacity-building potential and collective well-being.

For social-welfare liberals and small-government-loving libertarians alike, commonwealth entrepreneurship represents a unique, civic-minded initiative that engages our better angels and most industrious sensibilities to address matters that traditional for-profit entities, government agencies, and charitable organizations have not been able to do individually or collectively to date.

Unlike the usual framing of social entrepreneurship, commonwealth enterprises go beyond merely implementing a modus operandi that is implicitly socially responsible; it signifies the desired outcome. In other words, it's not just about good intentions, but meaningful outcomes. Embracing social enterprise, social entrepreneurship, and principles around the triple bottom line (one that integrates financial, environmental, and social gains) is only useful as long as we acknowledge the existence, relevance, and problematic nature of invisible capital.

We know that invisible capital is a mixed bag—that some assets are earned and others are claimed as the bitter fruit of inequality that inherently benefits one group over another. Commonwealth entrepreneurship elevates the social element of the triple bottom line from a vital dimension of an enterprise to the litmus test for success. Walmart is the largest provider of organic food in the United States. It also has one of the greenest footprints of any retailer in the world. Additionally, its philanthropic arm donates more money than the GDP of some developing nations. However, in the final analysis, if such businesses' toll on local communities impairs their socioeconomic sustainability, then the triple bottom line is too low a standard.

For every job Walmart creates in a community, nearly two are permanently destroyed.[13] Worse, the new jobs are not necessarily better or more secure than the jobs that have been lost. Job creation is good. But full-time, living-wage jobs that include decent benefits for employees in safe, clean, and nondiscriminatory workplaces should be a no-brainer.

Commonwealth entrepreneurship is not aspirational, it is prescriptive in nature. Simply put, its key threshold is whether the enterprise improves the broad sustainability of the community in which it operates—including the internal community of stakeholders without which the enterprise could not survive. For example, consider this announcement:

Behemoth Pacific—BPac for short—is a multinational general services corporation whose largest clients include various U.S. federal agencies and the governments of various Pacific Rim nations. It has been hit by bad press for the past several years because of questionable management decisions. In reinventing itself, it has embraced a triple-bottom-line approach to its business by 1) reducing its corporate eco-footprint and 2) creating the BPac Foundation to help needy children with serious medical conditions. It has also created a profit-sharing plan for its employees and rolled out a diversity-training program and an aggressive hiring initiative to recruit talented candidates of color from historically Black colleges and universities (HBCUs). Lastly, related to its outreach to underserved communities, the company has initiated a procurement program to groom vendors with Minority and Women Business Enterprise (M/WBE) certifications. In fact, BPac is helping current and prospective vendors produce greener products.

On the surface, all of these initiatives look honorable, quite promising, and well intentioned. Certainly, Behemoth Pacific is now an enterprise embracing a triple bottom line. The problem? BPac creates chemicals that make asbestos look like cotton candy and the most "intelligent" and lethal land mines ever built. If BPac's business model and product offerings are so heinous, does it really matter how green or how inclusive it is?

Building community wealth is paramount at a time when it has become increasingly hard for the average family to grow household wealth through homeownership, investment in real estate or financial vehicles, and traditional business formation—the three most popularly promoted means of personal wealth creation.

Now that you know how invisible capital influences business viability, you can also see how commonwealth entrepreneurship adds value to prospective entrepreneurs and their advocates. It is both a philosophical and highly practical framework that allows prospective and nascent entrepreneurs to significantly improve their chances of

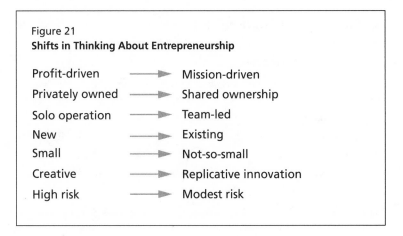

Figure 21
**Shifts in Thinking About Entrepreneurship**

| | |
|---|---|
| Profit-driven | Mission-driven |
| Privately owned | Shared ownership |
| Solo operation | Team-led |
| New | Existing |
| Small | Not-so-small |
| Creative | Replicative innovation |
| High risk | Modest risk |

building enterprises that will survive and flourish in a perilously high-risk field of endeavor.

How does commonwealth enterprise increase enterprise viability for entrepreneurs? If done right, the pursuit of financial outcomes that benefit the enterprise's stakeholders will be bolstered by invaluable core decisions to create organizational strengths where most conventional start-ups have weaknesses.

But we must also consider matters in addition to the *who* and the *how*. *Why* and *where* are vital considerations as well.

### Putting the Virtuous Cycle on Fast Spin

In 2008, Moody.com's chief economist, Mark Zandi, conducted a study to determine the types of stimulus projects that provided the biggest bang for the buck. At the top of the list was a program that may surprise millions of unsuspecting Americans: food stamps.[14] For every taxpayer dollar spent on food stamps for needy families, $1.73 circulated into our battered economy. The next most cost-effective use of stimulus funds was the extension of unemployment benefits, which for every dollar spent would yield $1.64—compared to a measly 33 cents for every dollar spent on tax breaks for "small businesses" by allowing companies to accelerate depreciation. (After all, if your business isn't making any money, a tax break is worthless.)

This study confirmed the importance of the virtuous cycle, the process by which value is created that in turn creates more value over and over again. It is the rare positive example of a self-fulfilling prophecy—one based on bottom-up investment rather than trickle-down trickery. The vicious cycle, on the other hand, allows businesses to grow "too big to fail," then uses taxpayer money to keep them afloat, still bloated, precariously operating until they eventually fail at our great mutual expense. But presumably on someone else's watch.

The relationship of the multiplier effect to commonwealth enterprises is still speculative and will require significant research to confirm. However, there are three areas of strategic concentration that we should keep our eyes on as more data become available.

### Broad Yield

Broad-yield enterprises are those ventures that can most feasibly produce the greatest breadth of net economic, social, and environmental impact on a given community. An extreme example would be a workers' cooperative that hires disabled veterans to assemble and install solar panels on remediated Superfund sites for public housing units, urban public school systems, and government facilities.

This is the picture of broad yield. The enterprise is worker owned and its employees therefore share in the fruits of the labor. And their work benefits not just themselves and their customers, but larger communities as well as the environment. It is not just the *greenness* of the products they produce and install, but the sustainability of the business model, its organizational structure, and its overall mission to create community assets that make it a truly broad-yield commonwealth enterprise.

### Rapid Scale

Rapid scale is not the same as "high scale." Highly scalable businesses tend to be technology-focused companies like Google, Amazon, eBay, eTrade, or Craigslist. Their capacity to expand is exponentially greater than that of brick-and-mortar companies due to the power and elasticity of digital technology, where traditional issues of material scarcity and scale are no longer as relevant as they were in the pre-Internet era.

Rapid scale, however, suggests that there are conventionally low-scale operations that, when strategically aggregated, can grow quickly to a scale that offers their stakeholders clear benefits that small, one-location outfits rarely do.

Across the country there are two-seat barbershops operating as neighborhood-based sole proprietorships that offer low-wage work for the underemployed and self-employed. But for many communities, barbershops are more than just storefront operations; they are social hubs and safe havens for local residents. An initiative to build rapid-scale commonwealth enterprises could start by consolidating select establishments to reduce overhead, provide living wages and employee benefits, and offer management training programs for their respective founders along with apprenticeships and incentives to attain additional formal education.

Such businesses are staples of virtually every local urban economy, yet few entrepreneurs who stay on the right side of the law make a good living or can afford to hire full-time, salaried employees—particularly in economically distressed neighborhoods where there would be many applicants per job opening for opportunities to earn a living wage.

### Post-Flux

Our government has bailed out massive corporations that many people believe did not deserve (or need) to be bailed out. Moreover, despite government's intervention, the writing is on the wall: some of the corporate giants that for generations were household names will be relegated to the history books in the coming years. Progressives hope that the entire health insurance industry will be dissolved if a single-payer health care system is ever adopted. Conservative politicians and their adherents have repeatedly called for lopping off entire federal agencies such as the Departments of Education and

Commerce, the Internal Revenue Service, the Environmental Protection Agency, and, yes, the Small Business Administration. President Obama's very own (initial) nominee for Secretary of Commerce, the senior senator from New Hampshire, Republican Judd Gregg, had in 1995 voted to abolish the very same agency he almost became the head of in 2009.[15] The aftermath of these massive changes would certainly be felt in the markets affected by these sweeping decisions, but more importantly by the people who would have been employed by the eviscerated agencies.

Post-flux enterprises would be entities established intentionally to rehire, retrain, and reinvigorate those portions of our labor force that would otherwise be cast aside if "free markets" did not in fact take care of them the way free enterprise proponents so often claim. Moreover, post-flux firms would innovate highly opportunistic business models that grow out of the gaping holes left behind by decimated industries and that emerging markets might create in their wake.

Back when it was all the rage to break new world records for the number of poor young nonviolent offenders we could lock away in concrete cells for whole lifetimes, the Prison-Industrial Complex became one of the most thriving industries in the U.S. and an economic boon for rural communities across the country. Today it seems that the business model that motivated the U.S. to become the biggest incarcerator of people on Earth isn't so economically sustainable. As it turns out, it costs more to house inmates than to educate our children. And when we're already competing (poorly) against much larger populations of skilled workers in India and China, relegating a growing percentage of our poorest children to lives behind bars doesn't make a whole lot of sense to the geniuses who thought this would be a sustainably high-growth industry (like credit default swaps).

What if one such post-flux enterprise began converting abandoned prisons into factories that actually manufactured products other than better-trained criminals? What if the solar panels that were assembled and installed by the disabled veterans were actually manufactured in the U.S. in facilities that once recycled inmates, but were converted into high-powered engines of a burgeoning green economy? We can look no further than the industry-made ecological catastrophe along the Gulf Coast in 2010 to see the tragic consequences of myopic profit maximization. Beyond the coastal communities ravaged for possibly generations to come is the very pressing reality that local economies there may be irreparably damaged. The business owners—most notably, proprietors of multigenerational shrimping outfits—may no longer be able to make a living the way their parents and grandparents did before them. Indeed, there is no better example of the type of community-oriented people—workers, not souless corporations—who could most benefit from a post-flux bailout.

How we apply our collective energies to these areas of strategic concentration for commonwealth entreprenuership is where invisible capital comes back into play. Remember, commonwealth enterprises and the kind of entrepreneurship they entail are envisioned to be far more viable than their conventional counterparts because the key predictors of business success are incorporated into their design.

The irony here is that commonwealth enterprises both by definition and in operation transcend the narrow prism of success. They instead take into account holistic, community-focused sustainability while bolstering their chances of surviving and thriving based on the most conventional measures.

### Making the Invisible Visible

It's up to us to embrace, promote, and build enterprises and their stakeholders—stakeholders who at least indirectly include us—toward achieving their goals by helping them leverage invisible capital.

We can do this individually and collectively in two very concrete but seemingly conflicting ways. First, we can help prospective and nascent entrepreneurs build invisible capital—particularly those who are drawn to commonwealth entrepreneurship. Second, we can shed light on those aspects of invisible capital that promote enduring inequities that are not born of anything within any individual entrepreneur's control.

Invisible capital's forces are largely unseen, even though they are hidden in plain sight. They are camouflaged by myth, deception, and fallacy, by memes like the American Dream, or by the belief that we already have a level playing field. Willful ignorance is its greatest facilitator.

The willfully ignorant among us don't want to know what they don't know because they are in love with their chains. Complacency fuels their acceptance of captivity. They fear the real freedom of knowing the truth, because deep down they know that what they've accepted may not be real, may not be true, or, worse, may not be morally consistent with their professed values.

Those who deny the claims of invisible capital often say they believe in equal opportunity, but not in equal *outcomes*. Sure, they say, we believe that all men are created equal, but that doesn't mean they will or should end up equal. These folks like to say that some people are "naturally" better entrepreneurs than others, and they use successful entrepreneurs as examples of *better* entrepreneurs. They take effect for cause.

It's true that not all people have the same abilities, orientations, temperaments, and so on. I agree with Peter Drucker, however, who writes: "Everyone who can face up to decision-making can learn to be an entrepreneur and to behave entrepreneurially."[16] What prevents some from becoming successful entrepreneurs is the lack of—or squandering of—invisible capital. These are the forces we must shine light on and leverage for the public good. Ultimately, we must collaborate to convert invisible capital into *influence capital*—invisible capital leveraged for social change—with the same creativity and aplomb that our country is known for.

As the late author, social worker, and civil rights activist Whitney Young Jr. wrote, "Along with equal opportunity will go the opportunity to be equal." In this statement Young implied, not so subtly, that equal opportunity does not presume a societal commitment to ensure equal preparedness for opportunity. This combination of preparation and opportunity is how we often colloquially define luck or good fortune. Horatio Alger may even have fallen into this camp. Invisible capital insidiously allows us to mistake privilege and opportunity for talent and merit by obscuring who is being prepared to excel and whether they are given such an opportunity (or can feasibly create one).

Few people in recent years have written about this fiction as clearly and masterfully as Malcolm Gladwell. In his book *Outliers: The Story of Success*, he writes:

> I want to convince you that these kinds of personal explanations of success don't work. People don't rise from nothing. We do owe something to parentage and patronage. The people who stand before kings may look like they did it all by themselves. But in fact they are invariably the beneficiaries of hidden advantages and extraordinary opportunities and cultural legacies that allow them to learn and work hard and make sense of the world in ways others cannot. It makes a difference where and when we grew up. The culture we belong to and the legacies passed down by our forebears shape the patterns of our achievement in ways we cannot begin to imagine."[17]

But we do imagine a world in which these societal inheritances don't exist. As a nation, we have blindly followed the Gospel of Possibility despite the fact that our addiction to the rhetoric of self-reliance and self-improvement cannot mask the Old World structures the Puritans' progeny have yet to fully cast off.[18] This nation lacks no history of hard work or ingenuity in all quarters, yet disparities persist since its founding that highly correlate to race, gender, and class.

When we actually honor the rhetoric of our Founding Fathers (rather than their practice) and commit to providing equal opportunity to all, we have found that in just one generation, dramatic progress can be achieved. Due to the great social upheavals of the labor, civil rights, women's, environmental, and gay rights movements, racial and gender equality, reproductive freedom, religious pluralism, and marriage equality for Millennials are now well within their generation's social norms (aspired to if not wholly practiced).

This societal transformation came about at the cost of great struggle, both nonviolent and bloody. In each instance the change was demanded by a minority and gradually embraced by a majority, for reasons not always based on moral enlightenment. But one morally enlightened reason was this: an egalitarian society was not only worth striving for, it was the only way to make our country realize its potential to be a great nation.

The values of acceptance, inclusion, and fairness that permeated the various grassroots movements of the 1960s and 1970s are just as relevant to the changes that are so necessary within our current entrepreneurial sector. We can make those changes by ensuring that all aspiring entrepreneurs understand the powerful impact of invisible capital and learn how to leverage their own invisible capital to create real entrepreneurial opportunity for themselves and equal footing for future generations.

# Notes

## Preface

1. Donald Trump and Meredith McIver, *Trump 101: The Way to Success* (Hoboken, N.J.: Wiley, 2007).
2. Devah Pager and Bruce Western, *Race at Work: Race and Criminal Record in the NYC Job Market* (New York: New York City Commission on Human Rights, 2005).
3. See Peggy McIntosh, "White Privilege: Unpacking the Invisible Knapsack," http://usapetal.net/wpmu/eh226/2009/09/29/white-privilege-unpacking-the-invisible-backpack/.
4. To learn about equitable ways of structuring internships, please read Kathryn Anne Edwards and Alex Hertel-Fernandez, *Paving the Way Through Paid Internships: A Proposal to Expand Educational and Economic Opportunities for Low-Income College Students* (Washington, D.C.: Demos/Economic Policy Institute, 2010), www.demos.org/publication.cfm?currentpublicationID=8C31B63F-3FF4-6C82-55528BC2ED4AE0F1.
5. See www.sba.gov/advo/whc1.txt.

## Introduction

1. U.S. Census Bureau, 2007 County Business Patterns and 2007 Economic Census. See www.factfinder.census.gov.
2. Ibid.
3. The general size standard for a "small business concern" is fewer than 500 employees. However, the Small Business Administration imposes additional criteria based on the type of industry and a variety of other factors to determine a firm's eligibility for participation in federal procurement programs reserved for small business concerns. For details, see web.sba.gov/faqs/faqindex.cfm?arealID=15.

4. U.S. Census statistics, as reported in *Business Dynamics Statistics Briefing: High Growth and Failure of Young Firms* (Kansas City, Mo.: Kauffman Foundation, 2010). See www.kauffman.org/uploadedFiles/bds_high_growth_and_failure_4-6-09.pdf.

5. Rosalene Glickman, *Optimal Thinking: How to Be Your Best Self* (New York: John Wiley & Sons, 2002), 20–21.

6. A definition of capital based on political economist Henry George's *Progress and Poverty* (1871).

7. Alicia Robb et al., *An Overview of the Kauffman Firm Survey: Results from the 2004–2007 Data* (Kansas City, Mo.: Kauffman Foundation, 2009), 13.

8. See http://history.nasa.gov/moondec.html.

9. *The Racial Wealth Gap Increases Fourfold*, IASP Research and Policy Brief, May 2010.

10. Edward N. Wolff, *Top Heavy: The Increasing Inequality of Wealth in America and What Can Be Done About It*, 2d ed. (New York: New Press, 2002), 5–6.

11. EBITDA stands for *earnings before interest, taxes, depreciation, and amortization*. It is essentially the *real* bottom line for for-profit enterprises, also referred to as *operating cash flow*. For more information on the language of business, visit www.InvisibleCapital.com.

12. See www.census.gov/econ/sbo/.

13. U.S. Census Bureau, 2007 County Business Patterns and 2007 Economic Census.

14. Ibid.

15. Bill McKibben, *Deep Economy: The Wealth of Communities and the Durable Future* (New York: Holt, 2007),108–9.

16. Ibid., 7.

17. Ibid., 108.

18. Johanna Mair, Jeffrey Robinson, and Kai Hockerts, eds., *Social Entrepreneurship* (Basingstoke, UK: Palgrave Macmillan, 2006), 95.

## Chapter 1  Dreaming a Difficult Dream

1. Alicia Robb et al., *An Overview of the Kauffman Firm Survey: Results from the 2004–2008 Data* (Kansas City, Mo.: Kauffman Foundation, 2010).

2. See, www.hernandezcollegeconsulting.com/ivy-league-admission-statistics-2009.

3. U.S. Census Bureau, 2007 County Business Patterns and 2007 Economic Census.

4. Ibid.

5. Ibid.

6. U.S. Census Bureau; Department of Labor, Bureau of Labor Statistics.

7. U.S. Census Bureau, Annual Economic Surveys, 2007 Nonemployer Statistics.

8. Vivek Wadhwa et al., *The Anatomy of an Entrepreneur: Family Background and Motivation* (Kansas City, Mo.: Kauffman Foundation, July 2009).

9. Secretary of Defense Donald Rumsfeld, press conference at the Pentagon, November 27, 2006; www.defense.gov/transcripts/transcript.aspx?transcriptid =2636.
10. Robb et al., *Overview of the Kauffman Firm Survey: Results from the 2004–2008 Data*, 15.
11. *Venture Impact: The Economic Importance of Venture Capital–Backed Companies to the U.S. Economy*, 5th ed. (New York: NVCA–National Venture Capital Association, 2009), 2.
12. U.S. Census Bureau, *Business Dynamics Statistics Briefing: High Growth and Failure of Young Firms, 2009*.
13. "America's 150 Largest Family Businesses," *Family Business Magazine*, August 24, 2009.
14. U.S. Census Business QuickFacts, 2008.
15. See www.nytimes.com/2010/06/02/opinion/02reich.html?_r=1&hp.
16. U.S. Census, Survey of Business Owners (SBO), Characteristics of Businesses: 2002, 2.
17. Timothy Bates, "Survival Patterns among Franchises & Non-Franchises Started in 1986/87," research study prepared for the Small Business Administration, 1996.
18. See www.directselling411.com/about-direct-selling/about-dsa/.
19. Nadine A. Thompson and Angela E. Soper, *Values Sell: Transforming Purpose into Profit Through Creative Sales and Distribution Strategies* (San Francisco: Berrett-Koehler, 2007).
20. James A. Muncy, "Ethical Issues in Multilevel Marketing: Is It a Legitimate Business or Just Another Pyramid Scheme?" *Marketing Education Review*, vol. 14, no. 3 (Fall 2004).

## Chapter 2    The Landscape of Modern American Enterprise

1. Ray Smilor, *Daring Visionaries: How Entrepreneurs Build Companies, Inspire Allegiance, and Create Wealth* (Boston: Adams Media, 2001).
2. Peter Drucker, *Innovation and Entrepreneurship* (Burlington, Mass.: Butterworth-Heinemann, 1985), 19.
3. Robert F. Hébert and Albert N. Link, *A History of Entrepreneurship* (New York: Routledge, 2009), 102–3.
4. Malcolm Gladwell, "The Sure Thing," *The New Yorker*, January 18, 2010, 24–29.
5. Ibid., 25.
6. Ibid., 27.
7. Jianwen Liao and Harold Welsch, *Handbook of Entrepreneurial Dynamics: The Process of Business Creation* (Thousand Oaks, Calif.: Sage, 2004), 188–95.
8. Max Weber, *The Protestant Ethic and Capitalism*, trans. Talcott Parsons (New York: Scribners, 1930 [1905]).

9. Howard Zinn, *The People's History of the United States: 1492 to Present* (New York: HarperCollins, 2005).

10. International Labor Organization; see www.boston.com/news/world/europe/articles/2007/09/03/study_us_workers_are_worlds_most_productive/.

11. Robb et al., *Kauffman Firm Survey, 2004–2008*, April 2009.

12. U.S. Census Bureau, USA QuickFacts, 2008.

13. U.S. Census Bureau, 2004.

## Chapter 3  Invisible Capital Exposed

1. Adapted from the quotation widely attributed to former Dallas Cowboys head coach Barry Switzer and popularized by the late governor of Texas, Ann Richards, who used it to describe former president George H.W. Bush at the 1988 Democratic National Convention.

2. Not surprisingly, Kiyosaki appears to remain silent on the curious timing of his rise to *New York Times* bestseller status not long after allying himself with multilevel marketing giant Amway's Quixtar subsidiary, which "encouraged" its many members to buy his books. For a critique of Kiyosaki's work, see John T. Reed's analysis at www.JohnTReed.com/kiyosaki.html.

3. As I like to remind my clients and others, ideas are not patentable. The best way to protect them is not to share them with people you don't trust.

4. Timothy L. O'Brien, *TrumpNation: The Art of Being The Donald* (New York: Warner/Business Plus, 2005), 214.

5. Pierre Bourdieu, "The Forms of Capital," in J. Richardson, ed., *Handbook of Theory and Research for the Sociology of Education* (Westport, Conn.: Greenwood, 1986).

6. Robert Putnam, "Bowling Alone: America's Declining Social Capital," *Journal of Democracy* 6:1 (January 1995): 65–78.

7. Mutual aid associations and the like were also established by, among other groups, rural and African American communities during the nineteenth century and later.

8. Michael Gerber, *The E-Myth Revisited: Why Most Small Businesses Don't Work and What to Do About It* (New York: HarperCollins, 1995).

9. Ibid., 16.

10. Hernando de Soto, *The Mystery of Capital: Why Capitalism Triumphs in the West and Fails Everywhere Else* (New York: Basic Books, 2006), 224–25.

11. Tom Hertz, "Understanding Mobility in America," American University, Center for American Progress, April 26, 2006.

12. Jeffrey R. Gates, *The Ownership Solution: Toward a Shared Capitalism for the 21st Century* (Reading, Mass.: Perseus, 1998), 23.

13. Adam Smith, *An Inquiry into the Nature and Causes of the Wealth of Nations*, Book II, Chapter 1 (London, 1776).

14. Henry George, *Progress and Poverty*, 23.

15. Martin Ruef, Howard E. Aldrich, and Nancy M. Carter, "The Structure of Founding Teams: Homophily, Strong Ties, and Isolation among U.S. Entrepreneurs," *American Sociological Review*, vol. 68, no. 2 (April 2003): 195–222.

16. Ibid., 217–18.

17. Ibid., 202.

18. Timothy Bates, *Race, Self-Employment and Upward Mobility: An Illusive American Dream* (Baltimore: Johns Hopkins University Press, 1997), 121.

19. U.S. Census Bureau, 2007 Economic Census, Survey of Business Owners.

20. Adrienne P. Samuels, "Guess Who Sells Your Weave?" *Ebony*, May 2008.

## Chapter 4  Democratizing Entrepreneurial Opportunity

1. Jessica Gordon Nembhard, "Cooperative Ownership in the Struggle for African American Economic Empowerment," *Humanity and Society*, vol. 28, no. 3 (August 2004): 298–321.

2. For more information on innovative organizational structures, check out www.InvisibleCapital.com.

3. Gar Alperovitz, *America Beyond Capitalism: Reclaiming Our Wealth, Our Society, Our Liberty and Our Democracy* (New York: Wiley, 2006), 70.

4. Gates, *Ownership Solution*, 22.

5. Scott A. Shane, *The Illusions of Entrepreneurship: The Costly Myths That Entrepreneurs, Investors, and Policy Makers Live By* (New Haven, Conn.: Yale University Press, 2010).

6. Ibid.

7. Nassim Nicholas Taleb, "Learning to Expect the Unexpected," *New York Times*, April 8, 2004; see www.edge.org/video/dsl/taleb.html.

8. Nassim Nicholas Taleb, "The Fourth Quadrant: A Map of the Limits of Statistics," *Edge/The Third Culture*, at www.edge.org/3rd_culture/taleb04/taleb_index.html.

9. Lawrence Mishel, "CEO-to-Worker Pay Imbalance Grows," Economic Policy Institute, www.epi.org, June 21, 2006.

10. Steven Hipple, "Self-Employment in the United States: An Update," *Monthly Labor Review*, July 2004.

11. Ibid.

12. Josh Harkinson, "Chamber Rejects Use of Term '3 Million Members,'" *Mother Jones*, October 23, 1999.

13. Log Cabin Republicans are a group within the Republican Party whose members are openly gay; LGBTQ stands for lesbian, gay, bisexual, transgender, and queer.

14. For a comprehensive list of people and groups who tell it like it is (and those who don't), check out www.InvisibleCapital.com.

15. See www.census.gov.

16. See www.census.gov/econ/sbo/.

17. Michael K. Brown and David Wellman, *Whitewashing Race: The Myth of a Color-Blind Society* (Berkeley: University of California Press, 2005), 75.

18. Jesse Washington, "'Black Power' Establishment Faces Tough Challenges," Associated Press, November 18, 2009.

19. Fairbank, Maslin, Maullin, Metz & Associates, "Executive Summary of American Dream Survey" (February 2010).

20. The 2008 Kauffman Firm Survey overview provides a range of illuminating information on how nascent entrepreneurs raise funds. Also visit www.InvisibleCapital.com for more information on this subject.

21. Scott A. Shane, "Angel Groups: An Examination of the Angel Capital Association Survey," Angel Capital Association, 2008.

22. To learn more about business incubators, please visit the website of the National Business Incubator Association at www.nbia.org/ and www.InvisibleCapital.com for related resources and information.

## Chapter 5  Reframing Entrepreneurial Success ... and Failure

1. Lynn Sweet, "First Lady Michelle Obama's Rollout: First FLOTUS Visit to Interior Dept. since Eleanor Roosevelt," *Chicago Sun-Times*, February 9, 2009.

2. Organization for Economic Co-operation and Development, *OECD Factbook 2010: Economic, Environmental and Social Statistics*, Public Finance: Taxes on the average worker (Paris: OECD Publishing, 2010); see also www.oecd.org/document/34/0,3343,en_2649_34533_44993442_1_1_1_1,00.html.

3. Alicia Robb and Robert Fairlie, *Race and Entrepreneurial Success: Black-, Asian- and White-Owned Businesses in the United States* (Cambridge, Mass.: MIT Press, 2008), 5.

4. Telephone interview with Prof. Rob Fairlie, May 20, 2010.

5. Alicia Robb and Susan Coleman, *Characteristics of New Firms: A Comparison by Gender* (Kansas City, Mo.: Kauffman Foundation, January 2009).

6. Shane, *Illusions of Entrepreneurship*, 11–12.

7. See www.ur/mich.edu/0708/Apr07_08/11.php.

8. NVCA website: http://www.nvca.org/index.php?option=com_content&view=article&id=119&Itemid=147.

9. John Talberth, Clifford Cobb, and Noah Slattery, *The Genuine Progress Indicator 2006: A Tool for Sustainable Development* (Oakland, Calif.: Redefining Progress, 2007).

## Chapter 6  Toward Commonwealth Entrepreneurship

1. David C. Korten, *Agenda for a New Economy: From Phantom Wealth to Real Wealth* (San Francisco: Berrett-Koehler, 2010).

2. John McKnight and Peter Block, *The Abundant Community* (San Francisco: Berrett-Koehler, 2010), 18–25.

3. Talberth, Cobb, and Slattery, *The Genuine Progress Indicator 2006*, 3.

4. Bruce Ackerman and Anne Alstott, *The Stakeholder Society* (New Haven, Conn.: Yale University Press, 1999).

5. Robb et al., *An Overview of the Kauffman Firm Survey 2004–2008*, 13.

6. See, for example, her recent book, written with Amy R. Poteete and Marco A. Janssen, *Working Together: Collective Action, the Commons, and Multiple Methods in Practice* (Princeton, N.J.: Princeton University Press, 2010).

7. See www.waynevisser.com/book_bf_chap6_beyond_growth.pdf.

8. John de Graaf, David Wann, and Thomas H. Naylor, *Affluenza: The All-Consuming Epidemic* (San Francisco: Berrett-Koehler, 2005).

9. See www.HappyPlanetIndex.

10. See www.RProgress.org.

11. Jessica Gordon Nembhard, "Cooperative Ownership in the Struggle for African American Economic Empowerment," *Humanity and Society*, vol. 28, no. 3 (August 2004): 298–321.

12. Ed Diener and Robert Biswas-Diener, *Unlocking the Mysteries of Psychological Wealth* (Malden, Mass.: Blackwell, 2008).

13. McKibben, *Deep Economy*, 106.

14. See http://money.cnn.com/2008/01/29/news/economy/stimulus_analysis/index.htm.

15. See www.usatoday.com/news/washington/2009-02-03-gregg_N.htm.

16. Drucker, *Innovation and Entrepreneurship*, 25–26.

17. Malcolm Gladwell, *Outliers: The Story of Success* (New York: Little, Brown, 2008), 19.

18. Roberto Mangabeira Unger and Cornel West, *The Future of American Progressivism: An Initiative for Political and Economic Reform* (Boston: Beacon, 1999), 18.

# Acknowledgments

Before I coined the term "invisible capital," I used the term "digital capital" to represent more or less the same thing, but relegated to the inequality of opportunity I perceived in the online world.

Since the 2004 presidential election, I have spoken publicly and consistently about how individuals' "digital capital" in the political blogosphere has been virtually invisible and why we needed to bring these advantages to light in order to understand how they have influenced the experiences, mobility, and participation of different groups of citizens of the Internet—aka "netizens."

The more I explored this idea with friends and colleagues, the more I realized that what I was talking about transcended social media or participatory journalism, and that these hidden assets were essentially forms of what I would later call "invisible capital."

It is in that spirit of transparency, accountability, and sharing that I would like to first acknowledge the abundant invisible capital that I was born with and have acquired over the first forty years of my life. Indeed, if it were not for this wealth of invisible capital, I assure you, this book would not have have been written nor published.

Of course, without the bulldog tenacity and single-mindedness of Johanna Vondeling, I would not have been encouraged to submit a book proposal to Berrett-Koehler in the first place. For her patience, foresight, and advocacy, I am truly grateful.

I would also like to thank Tanya Bridges for her wise legal counsel, and Simone White for introducing me to this young star.

Without the intellect, passion, and analytical gifts of my good friend and colleague, Roberto Lovato, I suspect what once was just a title of a single chapter would not have become the title of the book itself, as well as its central theme and what I anticipate will be the platform for a broader array of integrated endeavors.

There are also various organizations and institutions that I am thankful for being part of, including St. Ignatius College Prep, the LEAD Program in Business, Yale University, the Yale Black Alumni Network, the inaugural class of the Runners Club Entrepreneurial Program, the historic Sharp Street Memorial United Methodist Church's nonprofit Mt. Auburn Cemetery Corporation, the Baltimore Afro-American Newspaper Company, the Afro-Netizen community, German Marshall Fund of the U.S., The Media Consortium, the Progressive Communicators Network, ImprovEdge, Bread and Roses Community Fund, the Applied Research Center, the Poynter Institute, Harvard University's Berkman Center for Internet & Society, the Media Action Grassroots Network, Digital Justice Campaign, the Sustainable Business Network of Greater Philadelphia, Action-Mill, and the Ninth Ward Democratic Committee of Philadelphia, which serves much of the wonderful community of Mt. Airy, of which I have grown so fond.

As a new member of the Berrrett-Koehler community of authors and other stakeholders, I have been in very good company and am appreciative of the yeoman's efforts of Steve Piersanti, Jeevan Sivasubramaniam, Rick Wilson, Dianne Platner, and Mike Crowley, to name a few. Also, I am indebted to the editorial wizardry of Jo Ellen Green Kaiser and Steven Hiatt, and to the creative talents of Ian Shimkoviak, who designed a simply fabulous book cover, as well as to my dear friend and designer extraordinaire, Erin Shigaki.

I would also like to recognize the people who took the time and effort to substantively review, critique, and at times challenge elements of my manuscript: Mal Warwick, Cheryl Dorsey, Jay Rao, Shauna

Shames, Aura Bogado, David Korten, Jeff Scheuer, Lew Daly, Julie Kimmel, Marilyn Lambert, and James "Scootie" Bruce.

My short, but highly productive time as a member of the Princeton community has been that much more rewarding because of the support of Joan Girgus, Valerie Smith, Chris Paxson, Mark Watson, Paul Frymer, Leslie Gerwin, Steven "Zik" Adams, Deborah Kaple, Mary Beth Bellando, Rita Alpaugh, Paul DiMaggio, and the entire business office staff of the Woodrow Wilson School.

To my many muses: Elijah Anderson, Freager S. Williams, Donna Aiken, Michael Hayes, Darrell Williams, Karen Murphy, Audrey Petty, Karilyn Crockett, Eric Rigaud, Lorrin Thomas, Al Tillery, Gerry L. Davis, Safir Ahmed, John H. Morris Jr., William Brown, and the late great Okokon Okon III.

For a passionate and inveterate networker, few things are harder for me than devising a short list of people who have touched me in one way or another. However, no such list could be complete without mentioning the following names: Michael Ashley, Aspen Baker, Adi Bemak, Eva Blanco, James and Barbara Bowman, Chris Bradie, Christabel Nsiah Buadi, Patricia Casasola, Jennifer Cordero, LaFern Cusack, Byron Davis, Gerry and Anna Davis, Saundra Dougherty, Michael Eric Dyson, Kety Esquivel, Myrna Everett, Isaac Ewell, Phyllis Finch, Bill Generett, Nicholas Gowen, Vance Guidry, James Harris, Jerome Harris, Jean Harvey, Van Jones, Anthony Joseph, David Kairys, Paulette Kamenecka, Adam Karr, Bo Kemp, Phil LaMarr, Monique Long, Antje Mattheus, Tonie Mingo, Ako Mitchell, Tram Nguyen, Raimundo Nonato Moreira, Rob Okun, Dionne Otey, Todd Perry, Stacie Purdie, Kira Reed, Julieanna Richardson, Anike Robinson, Dee Robinson, Steven Rogers, Borracha Santana, Liz Scott, Rinku Sen, Shannon Shepherd, Rolf Skyberg, Linda Stout, Lorrin Thomas, Nate Thompson, Kevin Valentine, Scott Walker, and Linda Yudin.

Also: Muhammad Abdullah, Linda Baldwin, Al Barstow, Porter Bayne, Hilary Beard, Rich Benjamin, Julie Bergman Sender, Jessica Clark, Lark Corbeil, Gerald T. Davis, Brad deGraf, Sonya Donaldson, John Eldred, Allison Fine, Laura Flanders, Robert Fleming, Garlin

Gilchrist II, Susan Gleason, Robert Graff, Edward Gray, Van Hampton, Harold Haskins, Robert Holmes, Ina Howard-Parker, Ron Howell, Nike Irvin, lynne d johnson, Linda Jue, Steve Katz, Esther Kaplan, Thomas Lebens, Gail Leondar-Wright, Walter Lomax and family, Jim Lowry, Stephen Magowan, Nicco Mele, Toni Mingo, Shireen Mitchell, Chris Moore, Alex Moss, Ackneil Muldrow, Kevin Myles, Mark Pinsky, Kim Pearson, Chuck Pennacchio, Paul Porter, Dwight Raiford, Ric Ramsey, Andrew Rasiej, Ana Reyes, Kristina Rizga, Roy Roberts, Steven Rogers, James Rucker, Liza Sabater, Simran Sethi, Diane Shamis, Micah Sifry, Michael Strautmanis, Makani Themba-Nixon, Joe Torres, Kittie Watson, Shawn Williams, Jessica Valenti, Tracy van Slyke, David Whettstone, Maya Wiley, and Deanna Zandt.

I am so fortunate to have elders in my life to whom I owe so much and hold in such high regard, including my cousins Rufus Robinson Jr. and Carol Matthew, as well as the following heroes of mine who are nearing or far past 100 years of age: my great-uncle, Louis "Mike" Rabb and my great-aunt Sister Constance Murphy.

I am also truly thankful for the constant encouragement of my favorite radical epidemiologist Steve Whitman, the wonderful Perrys of Alabama, my aunt and uncles, cousins and extended family and the extended Duff clan who took me into their home as a young entrepreneur-in-training nearly twenty years ago.

There is also a fierce contingent of unofficial godmothers who have emboldened me since childhood with their unconditional love, wisdom, and sometimes a good, old-fashioned kick in the pants. They include Myra Frost, Joan Small, Billie Wright Adams, Beverly Hamilton Robinson, Lyndia Gray, Jetta Jones, and Arla Hightower, as well as other nurturers, including Lynn Small, Carolyn Armenta Davis, Maxine Leftwich, and Saundra Dougherty.

On the home front, no acknowledgments could be complete without honoring my late father, Dr. Maurice F. Rabb, Jr., a world-renowned eye surgeon, teacher, and innovative scientific researcher. He was quite possibly the most humble and gentle man I've ever known. You are sorely missed.

To my older brother, Maurice III, who was my business partner for many years, I can only say that as awe-inspiring as you are an inventor and computer scientist, your creativity is only surpassed by your integrity, decency, and lovingness as a father.

To my fabulous mother, Madeline Murphy Rabb, who remains a bold entrepreneurial artist—or perhaps an artistic entrepreneur—and who has built an ingenious art advisory firm that continues to inspire me. She is the person who taught me the importance of self-confidence, persistence, ingenuity, assertiveness, and old-school salesmanship. She is also the person who drilled into my head that fear of success is unacceptable, and that failure is both unavoidable and invaluable.

I have also been buoyed throughout my life by my late grandparents—most especially my maternal grandmother and grandfather, who were two of my greatest mentors. Madeline Wheeler Murphy was a journalist, community organizer, and Baltimore political icon. She was the person who encouraged me to write early and often—and to write to be understood, not to impress. She taught me about the power of language, community, and social justice—and how everything is political, "even when you flush the toilet!"

My grandfather, Judge William H. Murphy Sr., was a man obsessed with business, the law, and community wealth-building. His obsessions have greatly influenced my circuitous path to this point. I will always remember his admonition to me: "Don't tell me what you're gonna do, show me what you did!"

To my sons, Freeman Diallo and Issa, who fill my life with such joy, pride, and meaning, and who have become extraordinary little publicists, promoting my book with characteristic glee and enthusiasm.

My kindred spirit and co-parent, Imani Perry, who has inspired and supported me in so many invaluable ways over the last eleven years.

Lastly, I thank my ancestors—not just the entrepreneurs among them, but the ones who lived the African proverb, "I am because we are, therefore, we are because I am."

This book and the change it may spark are in homage to you.

# Resources

This book was written to help readers see the previously invisible and understand how unseen forces influence the landscape of opportunity that entrepreneurs and business owners must navigate.

I wrote *Invisible Capital* to be substantive, but accessible; short, but satisfying. That said, so much information exists that could not fit between the covers of this book.

At the Invisible Capital website, there is a treasure trove of information about the underpinnings of invisible capital; highly practical resources on entrepreneurship; facts, figures, and news about innovative policies, programs, initiatives, case studies, stories, trends, and opportunities. Additionally, you will find a whole host of useful tools, videos, and links for new and prospective entrepreneurs as well as their supporters and advocates.

I encourage you to visit www.InvisibleCapital.com, sign up to receive the free e-newsletter, and become an Invisible Capital community member.

# Index

# About the Author

Chris Rabb is a writer, consultant, and speaker on the intersection of entrepreneurship, media, civic engagement, and social identity. He is a visiting researcher at Princeton University's Woodrow Wilson School of Public and International Affairs as well as a Fellow at Demos, a nonpartisan public policy research and advocacy center in New York City. He is also a 2001 American Marshall Memorial Fellowship recipient awarded by the German Marshall Fund of the U.S. and has been a Fellow with the Poynter Institute since 2009.

Susan Beard Design

Mr. Rabb worked in the U.S. Senate as a legislative aide and as a writer, researcher, and trainer for the White House Conference on Small Business. He has worked in and on entrepreneurship from various vantage points, including founding a technology-based product design firm, running a nationally recognized nonprofit-based business incubator in Philadelphia and serving on a century-old family-owned newspaper business in Baltimore founded by an ancestor four generations ago.

Since his foray into the blogosphere in 2004 as one of the first group of bloggers to receive press credentials to cover a national political convention, he has become a regular panelist and speaker at conferences, universities, and corporate events nationwide, discussing such matters as participatory journalism, social media, civic engagement, and social justice.

He has written for various publications including *The Nation*, The Huffington Post and FastCompany.com, and has been covered by the *Wall Street Journal*, the *New York Times*, *Philadelphia Inquirer*, *ColorLines* magazine, *Mother Jones*, the *Chicago Tribune*, NPR, and BlogHer.

Mr. Rabb is a graduate of Yale College and earned an M.S. in organizational dynamics from the University of Pennsylvania. A native of Chicago and involved resident of the Mt. Airy community in Philadelphia, Chris is also a serial entrepreneur and avid genealogist whose work has been highlighted on National Public Radio and in various other local media outlets across the country since the 1990s.

For a more information on the author, visit www.ChrisRabb.com or email him at book@invisiblecapital.com.

# Dēmos

Dēmos is a non-partisan, public policy, research and advocacy organization founded in 2000. Headquartered in New York City, Dēmos works with advocates and policy-makers around the country in pursuit of four overarching goals:

- a more equitable economy with widely shared prosperity and opportunity;
- a vibrant and inclusive democracy with high levels of voting and civic engagement;
- an empowered public sector that works for the common good;
- and responsible U.S. engagement in an interdependent world.

### DEMOS FELLOWS PROGRAM

Dēmos is proud to be part of a progressive movement that is reshaping the way new ideas inform the public and policy debates, operating on a basis of shared responsibility and shared progress. We are working to incubate and execute new and diverse solutions to shared problems, and to offer long-rage goals that can create stability and prosperity for Americans and people around the world. Through the work of the Fellows Program, Dēmos supports scholars and writers whose innovative work influences the public debate about crucial national and global issues. The program offers an intellectual home and public engagement platform for more than 20 fellows from diverse backgrounds: emerging public intellectuals, journalists, distinguished public figures, and academics whose research can be used to inform the policy world.

## Berrett–Koehler
Publishers

Berrett-Koehler is an independent publisher dedicated to an ambitious mission: *Creating a World That Works for All*.

We believe that to truly create a better world, action is needed at all levels—individual, organizational, and societal. At the individual level, our publications help people align their lives with their values and with their aspirations for a better world. At the organizational level, our publications promote progressive leadership and management practices, socially responsible approaches to business, and humane and effective organizations. At the societal level, our publications advance social and economic justice, shared prosperity, sustainability, and new solutions to national and global issues.

A major theme of our publications is "Opening Up New Space." Berrett-Koehler titles challenge conventional thinking, introduce new ideas, and foster positive change. Their common quest is changing the underlying beliefs, mindsets, institutions, and structures that keep generating the same cycles of problems, no matter who our leaders are or what improvement programs we adopt.

We strive to practice what we preach—to operate our publishing company in line with the ideas in our books. At the core of our approach is stewardship, which we define as a deep sense of responsibility to administer the company for the benefit of all of our "stakeholder" groups: authors, customers, employees, investors, service providers, and the communities and environment around us.

We are grateful to the thousands of readers, authors, and other friends of the company who consider themselves to be part of the "BK Community." We hope that you, too, will join us in our mission.

### A BK Currents Book

This book is part of our BK Currents series. BK Currents books advance social and economic justice by exploring the critical intersections between business and society. Offering a unique combination of thoughtful analysis and progressive alternatives, BK Currents books promote positive change at the national and global levels. To find out more, visit **www.bkconnection.com**.

# Berrett–Koehler Publishers

A community dedicated to creating
a world that works for all

**Visit Our Website: www.bkconnection.com**

Read book excerpts, see author videos and Internet movies, read
our authors' blogs, join discussion groups, download book apps, find
out about the BK Affiliate Network, browse subject-area libraries of
books, get special discounts, and more!

**Subscribe to Our Free E-Newsletter, the *BK Communiqué***

Be the first to hear about new publications, special discount offers,
exclusive articles, news about bestsellers, and more! Get on the list
for our free e-newsletter by going to **www.bkconnection.com**.

**Get Quantity Discounts**

Berrett-Koehler books are available at quantity discounts for orders
of ten or more copies. Please call us toll-free at (800) 929-2929 or
email us at bkp.orders@aidcvt.com.

**Join the BK Community**

BKcommunity.com is a virtual meeting place where people from
around the world can engage with kindred spirits to create a world
that works for all. BKcommunity.com members may create their own
profiles, blog, start and participate in forums and discussion groups,
post photos and videos, answer surveys, announce and register for
upcoming events, and chat with others online in real time. Please join
the conversation!